WILLIAM GLOD

Why It's OK
to Make Bad Choices

Routledge
Taylor & Francis Group

NEW YORK AND LONDON

First published 2021
by Routledge
52 Vanderbilt Avenue, New York, NY 10017

and by Routledge
2 Park Square, Milton Park, Abingdon, Oxon, OX14 4RN

*Routledge is an imprint of the Taylor & Francis Group, an informa
business*

Library of Congress Cataloging-in-Publication Data
A catalog record for this book has been requested

ISBN: 978-0-367-19516-8 (hbk)
ISBN: 978-0-367-19517-5 (pbk)
ISBN: 978-1-003-04125-2 (ebk)

Typeset in Joanna MT Pro and DIN pro
by Apex CoVantage, LLC

Why It's OK
to Make Bad Choices

If we are kind people, we care about others, including others who tend to hurt themselves. We all have friends or family members who have potential but squander or even ruin their lives from things like drug abuse, unwise spending decisions, or poor dietary habits.

Concern for others often motivates us to endorse laws or private interventions meant to keep people from harming themselves even if that's what they want to do in the moment. However, it is far from clear that such paternalistic measures are, on net, benign, and they tend to violate an understanding that we should let adults make their own decisions.

In this little book, William Glod argues that it's OK to allow people to make bad choices. It's OK even if those choices risk causing a lot of harm. Most defenders of paternalism agree that some bad choices are not harmful enough to require laws to stop them. However, Glod goes further. He argues that some people might want – and *deserve* – the freedom to make truly bad choices because such freedom is the only way they can act responsibly. He also argues that some "bad" choices may not even be bad, even if we can't know with confidence a person's true desires. In addition, the book explores choices that are bad because they might impose high monetary costs on others, arguing that mandatory insurance may be a better solution than eliminating the choice. Finally, it explores the potential pitfalls of paternalistic laws and policies – and how unintended, costly consequences can sabotage the most well-intended plans.

Key Features

- Introduces key concepts for understanding paternalism and freedom of choice for undergraduates and general readers
- Discusses how many of our preferences are not easily understood by others, and shows how assumptions about true preferences can often backfire
- Explores ways in which people may want the freedom to make mistakes
- Examines the unintended consequences and associated problems of many paternalistic laws and regulations

William Glod is Senior Program Officer at the Institute for Humane Studies, an educational nonprofit affiliated with George Mason University in Arlington, Virginia.

Why It's OK: The Ethics and Aesthetics of How We Live

Philosophers often build cogent arguments for unpopular positions. Recent examples include cases against marriage and pregnancy, for treating animals as our equals, and dismissing some popular art as aesthetically inferior. What philosophers have done less often is to offer compelling arguments for widespread and established human behavior, like getting married, having children, eating animals, and going to the movies. But if one role for philosophy is to help us reflect on our lives and build sound justifications for our beliefs and actions, it seems odd that philosophers would neglect arguments for the lifestyles most people—including many philosophers—actually lead. Unfortunately, philosophers' inattention to normalcy has meant that the ways of life that define our modern societies have gone largely without defense, even as whole literatures have emerged to condemn them.

Why It's OK: The Ethics and Aesthetics of How We Live seeks to remedy that. It's a series of books that provides accessible, sound, and often new and creative arguments for widespread ethical and aesthetic values. Made up of short volumes that assume no previous knowledge of philosophy from the reader, the series recognizes that philosophy is just as important for understanding what we already believe as it is for criticizing the status quo. The series isn't meant to make us complacent about what we value; rather, it helps and challenges us to think more deeply about the values that give our daily lives meaning.

Titles in Series

Why It's OK to Want to Be Rich

Jason Brennan

Why It's OK to Be Of Two Minds

Jennifer Church

Why It's OK to Ignore Politics

Christopher Freiman

Why It's OK to Make Bad Choices

William Glod

Selected Forthcoming Titles:

Why It's OK to Get Married

Christie J. Hartley

Why It's OK to Love Bad Movies

Matthew Strohl

Why It's OK to Eat Meat

Dan C. Shahar

Why It's OK to Mind Your Own Business

Justin Tosi and Brandon Warmke

Why It's OK to Be Fat

Rekha Nath

Why It's OK to Be a Moral Failure

Robert Talisse

Why It's OK to Have Bad Grammar and Spelling

Jessica Flanigan

For further information about this series, please visit: www.routledge.com/
Why-Its-OK/book-series/WIOK

Contents

Acknowledgments

I have had discussions with and received comments from many people over the years on topics that ended up in this book. Their patient feedback has kept me from making many bad choices about what to include and how to argue for it. Any errors that remain are my own. I would like to thank the following colleagues and scholars, with apologies if I have accidentally overlooked anyone:

Jonny Anomaly, Anne Baril, Chris Boom, Piper Bringhurst, Bruce Brower, Ben Bryan, Trevor Burrus, Michael Cholbi, Thomas Christiano, Andrew Jason Cohen, Shane Courtland, Ryan W. Davis, Jakina Debnam, David Faraci, Jessica Flanigan, Chris Freiman, Jerry Gaus, Kalle Grill, Mark David Hall, Javier Hidalgo, Jeanne Hoffman, Pietro Intropi, Peter Jaworski, Mark LeBar, Keith Lehrer, Adam Lerner, Jimmy Lewis, Eric Mack, Alexei Marcoux, J.P. Messina, Jonathan Miles, Cecilia Orphan, Aaron Ross Powell, Maura Priest, Jonathan Quong, Greg Robson, Dan Russell, Dave Schmidtz, Lucia Schwarz, Danny Scoccia, Daniel Silvermint, Irina Soboleva, James Stacey Taylor, John Thrasher, Kevin Vallier, Chad Van Schoelandt, Mario Villarreal-Diaz, and Steven Wall.

I would also like to thank two anonymous reviewers for their many incisive and thoughtful comments on an earlier draft of this manuscript. Their feedback certainly made the book clearer and more integrated than it was initially.

Andy Beck at Routledge has been wonderfully supportive of the project throughout and has always promptly answered any questions I had along the way. He's an editor any author would want to have on board. Many thanks also to other staff and teams at Routledge – many whose names I don't know – for putting so much work into making sure this book was successful.

I'd also like to thank my past and current friends and colleagues at the Institute for Humane Studies who are too many to name, my personal best friends (Derrik, Jillian, Patrick, Tiff, William), and my mom and dad for their continued support and love. Without them, I would never have gotten this far.

Finally, this book is dedicated to the memory of my dear friend and sister, Leslie Glod Barnes (1968–2016).

Why read this book? Well, we're all likely to make bad choices on occasion, and one question is what should be done about it. Can the law stop you from making bad choices? Can your friends or family stop you? A stranger? So I hope you read this book to consider some things that perhaps you haven't thought about before. I think this book will be relevant to you! Why? For starters, I will try to show that some "bad" choices aren't really bad. And if they're not bad, they're OK! Other choices are indeed bad, but it's still OK for us to be free to make them. Yet other choices are bad but we don't always know they're bad until after we make them, so they are OK too. Some choices are potentially bad because they might harm others in addition . . . those may not be OK.

Your job is to show where I go wrong. Look out for where you think my arguments don't work or can be stronger, even if – *especially if* – you are inclined to agree with my conclusions. I can't pretend to provide a knockdown argument in these pages, and one thing I hope to avoid is coming across like I'm lecturing you. That is the last thing I want to do, since philosophy is best done as a discussion. Of course, I can't be here to chat with you in real time as you read along, so I've tried to make my words sound as if I'm there in the room with you. But please feel free to reply. Write in the margins – well, *only if* the book is yours. If you are outraged by something I'm defending, raise the issue with your friends or post questions on social media. Write a letter to the editor of your newspaper.

Here's the basic structure of the book: It's OK to make bad choices when you and others can learn from them, and they don't cause you **the major types of harms that concern paternalists** (Chapter 1). It's OK to make bad choices since **we can't assume that they are actually "bad" when evaluated in context** (Chapter 2). It's OK to have the freedom to make even strongly bad choices because it's not OK for people to stop you from making them **when you want this freedom for all your choices and/or having this freedom is a significant conception of your identity** (Chapter 3). It's OK to have the freedom to make even strongly bad choices because it's not OK for people to **assume** you are fine with coercive paternalism by **not *already* rejecting it** (Chapter 4). It's OK to have the freedom to make bad choices if they are **genuinely your choices** and not because of distorting cognitive or motivational issues, correction of which isn't readily under your awareness or control (Chapter 5). It's OK to have the freedom to make bad choices if *allowing* **such freedom does not impose undue costs** on others without their consent (Chapter 6). Finally, it's OK to have the freedom to make bad choices if *restricting* **such freedom would raise undue costs or harms to others or to those we aim to benefit** (Chapter 7). Chapter 8 concludes.

I've thought about the issue of making bad choices for a long time, but I don't have a monopoly on the truth. So challenge me – do not take what I write as if it were the final say. Alright, let's get started.

One

All of us have done things we later regret. Think of some things you've done that you wish you hadn't. Don't worry, I'm not trying to make you feel guilty. I'm just trying to illustrate that we sometimes stumble and make mistakes. Sometimes we hurt other people by running our mouths or breaking promises. When we see that we've hurt others, most of us feel guilt and remorse for the pain we have caused them and for not living up to a better version of ourselves. In this book, I will focus mainly on times in which our poor decisions, our bad choices, largely harm ourselves.

Why should you care about this issue? Because all of us often face opportunities to make bad choices. They might seem like good ideas at the time, or we might want to take a chance when we're not sure. Some believe that people should be free to make bad choices, to harm themselves, as long as it doesn't really harm others without their consent. The first few chapters of this book will be my attempt to defend this view against important objections. However, to defend this I will need to address a view called "coercive paternalism" – as distinct from "libertarian paternalism" or "nudging" – which may be more familiar to you. I'll say more about nudging later and in Chapter 5. Coercive paternalism (henceforth simply "paternalism") holds that it may sometimes be OK to forcibly intervene when a person is likely to do some action that will harm her overall, on balance, when any benefits that action brings her are outweighed by the costs that she faces from it. We might intervene simply by warning her about what she is doing, but the more interesting views of paternalism are ones that say it's permissible to interfere with her *even* if she is making a free and sufficiently informed choice to do something harmful to herself. I will say more about these views later.

Now you might be thinking: "If an adult chooses to do something bad to himself, why shouldn't he be free to do it, as long as it doesn't violate other people's rights or hurt them significantly? What business is it of someone else to intervene?" This is a common view, especially among Americans with their tradition of rugged individualism and "Don't Tread on Me" Gadsden flags. But one response is that we are imperfect and sometimes make dumb decisions that can have very bad consequences. We don't usually *intend* those consequences when we choose badly. A second response is that we often predictably feel regret at those decisions and would be grateful if someone had prevented us from making some of these bad choices. Perhaps our "future selves" would look back on some of the bad choices we made and, if only they could time travel, would let paternalists stop our earlier selves from making those choices.

Research in psychology has uncovered many ways in which we allegedly behave irrationally. For instance, our preferences are sometimes inconsistent (we may want to lose weight *and also* eat heaping piles of nachos). We make decisions in the heat of the moment that our better selves would wish we hadn't made. ("Did I really need that expensive new flat screen TV when I can barely afford my rent?") "Wishful thinking", also known as "optimism bias", tempts to us to think bad things won't happen to us when we act in risky ways ("I can smoke because cancer only affects poor and old people, not me!") We are weak-willed: I tell myself that I'm not going to eat dessert after dinner, but every single time I give in to temptation when I see the chocolate cake. We lose sight of how harms add up: the harm of one tobacco cigarette is negligible, but most smokers aren't thinking about how the tens of thousands of cigarettes they smoke over a lifetime accumulate into possibly severe harms.

We then regret making these bad choices and often we wish someone calmer with better sense had been there to at least talk us out of it, if not prevent us from making it altogether. You might be predictably grateful for someone stopping your impulsive flat screen purchase, or maybe for the law giving you a week's cooling-off period to return it for a full refund no questions asked. You might be grateful for a smoking ban 40 years later when you can still breathe and lift your grandkids. Think of your future self again. Think of the paternalist as *that* version of you. You could be grateful afterward for certain interventions in the same way you might thank your caretakers for enforcing a curfew in high school, thus keeping you out of the trouble you saw your other friends find at 2 a.m. Defenders of paternalism can point to these attitudes and suggest that perhaps you at your wisest really would have liked to be restricted even though you at your less wise didn't want it *at the time*. These attitudes also suggest that we don't judge our lives moment-to-moment. Rather, we look at the shape of how things go over a lifetime. There are no doubt many things I look back on and wish I had done differently.

So if we are imperfectly rational, and if people predictably tend to feel regret for making certain types of bad self-harmful choices, why *shouldn't* we have safeguards that lessen the likelihood that we will do such foolish things even as adults? Some defenders of paternalism think the state (at least in theory) can play a significant role through coercive laws, policies, and regulations.

Now some think we can have effective policies without needing force or the threat of force directed toward would-be self-harmers. This "libertarian paternalism" or "nudging" is probably the most common use of the term "paternalism" today. Nudging is the view that we can actually use people's biases to influence them to act in better ways. For example, we can manipulate people into eating healthier by putting the healthy food at eye level and making the less healthy food harder to notice or to reach.[1] This type of nudging involves what are called "framing effects" in that minor changes in how information is structured can have a significant influence on how people act. We can encourage people to save more for retirement by *automatically* enrolling them in retirement accounts, while allowing them to opt out, rather than requiring them to opt in first. This is because many people never get around to opting in and thus miss out on building retirement savings. But if they're automatically enrolled, then if they procrastinate and never opt out, most of them will benefit financially from their laziness!

Doctors who think patients should undergo a certain procedure can manipulate ordering effects by listing the doctors' preferred treatment first. Doctors can also use framing effects. For instance, patients told that they have a 9 in 10 chance of surviving a surgery will more likely opt for it than if the same patients are told that they have a 1 in 10 chance of dying. These statements mean the same thing logically, but they can influence people to act very differently! The idea here is that we have to arrange things or provide information in *some* way or another. There is no neutral way to present options, so we might as well do it in a way that tends to steer people toward healthier decisions than they might otherwise make, given their biases. But such nudges only aim to *influence* our behavior – unlike coercive paternalism, they do not aim to restrict our freedom to choose good or bad because we are still free to do whatever we prefer to do in that moment. A person who strongly prefers not to have surgery won't be strongly affected by the "9 out of 10" language.

Nudging may have other problems, discussion of which is beyond the scope of this book, but it doesn't restrict our freedom to make choices. I will say more about nudging in Chapter 5, but here it's important to note that some defenders of paternalism think nudging, while sometimes effective, often doesn't go far enough. They defend legal coercion, that is, physical force or its threat backed by the state. They argue that if certain choices are bad enough, people shouldn't be free to make them at all. Instead of steering people toward retirement savings by changing the default option to automatic enrollment, we should just by law require people to put aside a certain amount of their income. Instead of merely putting sugary food and drinks away from eye level or in the back of the store, we should heavily tax or even prohibit their sale. Instead of putting scary warning labels or images on cigarette packaging, we should heavily tax or ban cigarettes altogether. This book will focus on this more traditional, *coercive* type of paternalism, which is regaining some favor and some serious intellectual defenders with whom this book will spar.

The argument is that freedom to make bad enough choices just isn't valuable in these contexts. Why should anyone *want* the freedom to make really bad choices that they will likely later regret, choices that harm their overall interests and may even undermine their future freedom? People won't miss smoking if the law keeps them from ever taking up the habit, and current smokers will get used to the new order after enough time, even if they are frustrated or resentful at first. People change, and the thought is that this frustration and resentment will likely turn to relief if not gratitude as ex-smokers get older, wiser, and healthier than they would otherwise be. You might still think, however, that this is treating adults like young children, so to be fair I should pause and outline some arguments for why perhaps we shouldn't think of paternalism in that caricatured way.

TAKING PATERNALISM SERIOUSLY

First, the best defenders of paternalism stress that we are only talking about certain harmful behavior being up for intervention. (Note throughout that I will use "harm" to mean a setback to a person's overall interests. The word is not always used in this way, but we'd get too far off-track to pursue that issue.) Paternalists don't want to stop all risky and harmful behavior because that would be meddlesome and perhaps even counterproductive to learning. They think it's OK to make bad choices – as long as they aren't *too* harmful. I will argue in later chapters that they don't go far enough. We should have a wider scope to make even very bad choices, but first let's hear from the defenders of paternalism.

Usually for a harm to warrant paternalism, it will have at least two of three features: severity, immediacy, and irreversibility. Examples of severe and often irreversible (but not immediate) harms are diseases related to long periods of smoking or poor diet, or lack of retirement savings from years of excessive spending. Severe and immediate (but reversible) harms might be large sums of money lost from gambling, or injuries like broken bones from failing to wear protective equipment at a construction site. These are reversible of course because bones heal and people of working age and ability can normally make back money lost. Immediate and irreversible (but perhaps not severe) harms might include, say, face tattoos that lower one's ability to get an office job, or costly multi-year contracts with one's cellular service that turn out to be annoyingly bad deals. A harm that includes all three features would be whimsical suicide, that is, someone whose life is going pretty well but who decides – for no good reason – to kill themselves. (Contrast this with rational suicide to end great suffering from an incurable illness.)

Defenders of paternalism often argue that the types of harms outlined previously are the only candidates for restriction or prohibition. We might ban (or, if relevant, tax): smoking, sodas, certain fatty or sugary junk foods, gambling, and face tattoos ("Think before you ink"). We might require businesses not to adhere to certain contractual arrangements that tend to hurt non-savvy customers. We might require people to wear seat belts (as laws in most places currently do already). But serious defenders of paternalism don't want to intrude on every little bad thing we might choose, certainly not when the intervention would likely be worse or costlier than the bad thing itself, or when we and others can learn from our mistakes. Badness comes in degrees, after all. Mild harms may only have one of the three features mentioned earlier, and so are less likely to be apt targets of paternalistic laws.

A severe harm might be a failed marriage, but that is typically not immediate (it usually takes time for a couple to realize a particular marriage might have been a bad idea) and it's reversible (divorce can keep a bad marriage from being a life sentence). Immediate harms that are reversible and not severe include bellyaches from too much candy (you'll feel better in the morning) and bad haircuts (it'll grow out in a few weeks). Irreversible harms that aren't immediate or severe include minor hearing loss from years of playing one's rock albums loudly. Most defenders of paternalism think you should still be free to eat a bit too much ice cream, explore potentially bad romances, get cheap haircuts, and blast AC/DC from your earbuds. Even paternalists think it's OK to make these sorts of bad choices, if only because they're not catastrophic and it's not worth it to try stopping you.

A second claim for why we should not think paternalists aim to treat us as children is that people don't actually want to suffer these bigger harms, given everything else they value, their overall best interest. Many paternalists insist that any proper manipulation or interference they defend is not meant to reflect values held only by the paternalist and not by the intended target. Rather, paternalism is meant to help us all do what we ourselves would want to do if we were not saddled with biases, clouded judgment, hot emotions, and weak wills. If they sat you down and got you to really think through things, you could get a better and more informed perspective on whether and when you should engage in certain habits.

The perspective of that wiser version of yourself is what we're looking for in deciding whether to intervene with your less-wise self. You might get some pleasure out of smoking, to be sure, but prolonged cigarette use often takes several years off a person's life, and that person often lives out their final years with a lot of painful and debilitating health problems, like cancer or emphysema. Is the pleasure from the nicotine rush really worth the threat to everything else in your life that you value? You might get a similar rush from hitting the casino, but are heavy gambling debts worth it when you now face bankruptcy and bad credit for perhaps much of your life? (Wise advice: the house always wins in the long run.) Maybe your seat belt chafes you, but shouldn't you be forced by law to wear it so that, heaven forbid, you don't get in an accident that causes you mangled limbs, paralysis, or death?

Paternalists are not trying to impose their own view of the good life on you when you don't share that view. Rather, they are trying to relieve you of the burden of having to take responsibility for avoiding certain behaviors that shouldn't be allowed in the first place. You may be someone who smokes or gambles a lot, but those behaviors don't define you. Your life is made up of so much more than that. You are the person you are based on important things like your work, your relationships, and how you respond to adversity. It's not about how many Big Gulps you can drink in one week.

We want to be prudent and rational so that we can enjoy the things in life that really matter to us. The philosopher Adam Smith put it best when he wrote that people naturally desire not merely to be loved but to be "lovely".[2] We want to be the best versions of ourselves, not Homer Simpsons, and paternalism might help us aspire to that ideal by keeping our worst choices out of the picture. The presumption is that none of us want to be obese, sick, or poor. So why would we want to be free to eat junk, smoke, or go bankrupt in retirement? Freedom is valuable in itself and for the good things it can bring us, but not for major harms without compensating benefits. Paternalism can preserve our freedom to a large degree while saving us the trouble of having to fight harmful temptations ourselves, so that we can better get to where we want to go in life and avoid serious harms that we would likely regret.

COMMON OBJECTIONS TO PATERNALISM

I will now sketch five commonly cited problems with paternalism: it won't work, it is insulting or disrespectful, it imposes values, it violates rights, and it is likely to be misapplied or abused. Not everyone who objects to paternalism holds all five of these views, and some might only hold one or two. But defenders of paternalism, such as Jason Hanna, regard these as among the most common objections. By contrast, Hanna defends a view he calls "pro-paternalism", which he describes as follows:

> If the interests that would be served by intervention are weightier or more important than the interests (of the same person) that would be thwarted by intervention, then intervention advances this person's interests *on balance*, or as I shall say, is in her *best interest*.[3]

If some intervention would likely advance someone's overall interest, then Hanna claims it might be OK to intervene – it always provides a valid reason even if that reason isn't decisive or conclusive. He thinks that successfully replying to all five objections would be a major step toward showing that there is at least nothing *distinctively problematic* about pro-paternalism that other views we typically accept would not face as well. If we allow for these other views, why not allow for pro-paternalism too? Hanna adds: "[T]he claim that intervention is in a person's best interest implies that there is no alternative that would advance this person's interests to a greater extent."[4]

Paternalism won't work: There are several arguments along these lines, but here I will focus on the two strongest ones. First, some argue that paternalism won't work because people know their own good better than outside parties, and so interventions (especially by distant people such as government agents) will almost always end up doing more harm than good. We are almost always better at securing our own best interests because we are better placed to know what those interests are and how to control our decisions to secure them.

Second, paternalism won't work because it undermines individuality, which most of us (at least in liberal democracies) value highly through making our own choices. Both of these views were developed by John Stuart Mill in his famous 1859 book *On Liberty*. (If you haven't read it, it's in your best interest to add this book to your list.)

As for the first point, defenders of paternalism have plausible responses to the claim that people always more effectively secure their own best interests. Hanna writes:

> There are some cases in which a weak-willed individual admits that his choice is contrary to his well-being. . . . [In the case of smokers who have tried to quit and failed], the general presumption that the individual is the party most able to secure his best interest may not apply. Relatedly, individuals may be subject to temptation of a sort that leads them to ignore or downplay considerations that oppose the course of action toward which they are tempted. . . . Moreover, even if an individual has special expertise about his current tastes and desires, he may not have special expertise regarding the ways in which his tastes and desires will change in the future.[5]

Since we are sometimes weak-willed, since we sometimes fail to put forth enough effort to do what is in our best interest (even when we want to secure our best interest), it might be more effective for an outside party, one who isn't afflicted with weak will in this instance, to intervene.

In addition to weak wills, temptation often leads us to downplay the costs of making the tempting choice. Joe might only think about the sweet ride that sleek Maserati will be and how popular it might make him, while forgetting that he won't be able to afford groceries if he buys it. Perhaps outside parties who aren't facing Joe's temptation would find it wise to have a mandatory "cooling down" period in which Joe is not allowed to purchase the car that slick salesperson is pushing him to get. Given a couple of weeks, he may then have more time to think things through rather than act impulsively, and his temptation might fade.

Finally, people's tastes and desires change, so we should think about our future selves and not just our current ones. And we may be pretty bad at predicting what our future desires might be, especially if we are only focused on the here and now. Outside parties, who might be more aware that certain decisions predictably cause people to regret them down the road, would be better placed than the choosing individual to at least caution them if not interfere with certain predictably harmful and regrettable choices.

Maybe, however, paternalism doesn't work for a different reason – perhaps it always does harm to the target's individuality, that is, her ability to develop her unique talents and learn from her mistakes as needed. Paternalism frustrates a person's self-development and is thus wrong for that reason. Rather than being able to do her own thing in her own way, intervention sometimes forces her not to make her own choices, and that stunts her growth as a person and interferes with her ability to live *her own* life.

Defenders of paternalism have two responses, however. First, they can agree that individuality is an important part of our overall best interest, but surely it is only one part among others.[6] We also have interests in achieving our career goals, maintaining valuable relationships, having healthy psyches, and being safe enough from harm that we can enjoy pursuit of these interests. There may be times where sacrificing a bit of individuality would promote or protect these other interests. Bob enjoys alcohol and considers drinking to be a part of his identity as a party animal. However, it has turned into a problem. He now drinks in the morning (even having a beer for breakfast in the shower), at the office, and pretty much whenever he's awake but not driving. It has diminished his ability to work on projects he otherwise values. Booze occupies his thoughts, distracting him from things he used to enjoy. He has alienated some friends with blackout drunken tirades, and his sex life has suffered. Lately his anxiety has increased and he is nearing depression on seeing the problems his drinking has caused.

Let's say that raising the price of booze will lower Bob's consumption so that at least it's not quite the problem it has been. Perhaps drinking less would also make him more clearheaded and willing to get therapy. Have we set back Bob's interest in individuality by making it a bit harder for him to drink as much as he otherwise would? Perhaps, but we have probably helped serve his *overall* best interest through the alcohol tax. Besides, his party animal persona has taken him down a dark road that is not worth traveling – it may have started out fun but look where it's gotten him. It's not even clear that taxing alcohol or tobacco would diminish one's individuality. Hanna writes:

> An increase in the price of cigarettes, resulting from a tobacco blight, would appear to pose no great threat to our

self-development, even if it does effectively price some people out of the market. Why should we think any differently if the price of cigarettes were to increase as the result of a tax imposed for the purpose of deterring smoking?[7]

Defenders of paternalism can go further – perhaps some paternalism can even *help* protect or promote individuality itself! How so? Suppose that the reason many people smoke is because they started in their youth when their friends were doing it and they felt the need to fit in without really wanting to smoke. Conformity is the opposite of individuality! Perhaps by banning cigarettes (or at least tobacco advertisements making it look cool), we could create an environment where people are *less* prone to conform and more likely to develop their own unique tastes and talents.[8] (One might say the same about banning or regulating other forms of advertising too, such as fashion.) A world in which everyone says the same thing, dresses the same, and listens to the same music is a shopping mall in the suburbs, not a world marked by individuality.

Also note that even if skeptics could show that paternalism often does more harm than good to the target, that doesn't show that it's wrong in principle, as such, only that it's wrong when it doesn't work. And if we are confident that it sometimes does work, then it might be appropriate in those cases only.[9] Perhaps antipaternalists should instead try to show that paternalism is wrong *even if it works all the time*. That is, it's wrong to intervene even if doing so actually does help promote or protect that person's best interest. We turn now to three such arguments.

Paternalism is disrespectful or insulting: We can all agree that if someone is incapable of acting responsibly, or it's unclear whether they know that they are acting dangerously, it's OK to stop them. Our friend John Stuart Mill gave the example of a person who is about to cross a dangerous rotten old bridge but isn't aware of the danger. Say you're a bystander and don't have time to warn the person, but you do have time to grab him before he steps on the bridge. In this case, you are intervening for that person's best interest, and it doesn't seem wrong to do so because he (we assume) knew nothing about the risks of danger. In a real sense, the would-be crosser doesn't know what he's about to do, so it seems OK to restrain him at least until he is informed.

This example captures what is sometimes called **"soft" paternalism**, as distinguished from the **"hard" paternalism** we have been discussing so far. Let me pause to clarify how I'm using this distinction, since there are several senses of it in the literature. I will be using Joel Feinberg's sense of "soft paternalism", which holds that interference with a person's actions is permissible when those actions are nonvoluntary, or we lack sufficient evidence that the actions are voluntary. Here, soft paternalism is consistent with respecting a person's freedom and autonomy because nonvoluntary actions are not in his control – he is not freely acting when he performs them. For instance, if unconscious brain processes force me to think I must save the world by shoveling donuts in my mouth, I don't have the choice to continue or stop eating them. A person who stops these actions is acting in a soft paternalistic manner. Presumably I would not want to be out of control in this way, and stopping the action is consistent with respecting my freedom because I wasn't acting freely in the first place.

What's more controversial is when a person is capable of acting voluntarily and responsibly – he knows to a large degree what he's doing – but nonetheless freely makes bad choices. That is, he does so *willingly*, not from inability or ignorance.

Many defenders of hard paternalism argue that, even if a person is choosing to act self-harmfully – he knows what he's doing and is aware of the risks but downplays or ignores them – it might nonetheless be OK to stop him. This "hard paternalism" will be the focus of the book except for Chapter 5, where I discuss soft paternalism in greater depth.

Some skeptics of paternalism claim stopping capable adults from self-harmful behavior is disrespectful. When we stop young children from running into the road or overindulging on sweets, we are doing so because young children don't know any better. They haven't had the chance to learn how to judge risks or determine what is bad for them. Young children aren't yet capable of thinking about their long-term interests, so it's OK – in fact, it's a parent or guardian's duty – to look out for the child's interests until they are capable of looking out for themselves.

Things are different with adults because adults have a different status: they are usually able if not willing to do what young children can't. They are *at fault*, accountable, for their bad choices in ways young children usually are not. To force a competent adult to save for retirement, or to force him not to smoke, is to treat that adult as if he were a child. Such interventions fail to treat him with adequate respect as a person capable of making his own decisions, good or bad. They belittle his status as someone able to think for himself and decide what risks he is going to take, or so goes this charge of disrespect.

A related objection is that paternalism is insulting because it feels demeaning to an adult when another adult makes him do what he doesn't want to do. It expresses an elitist and snobby attitude when in fact we are all equals here. Just as we think fat-shaming and "mansplaining" are rude, we have to question the motives of people who might have too much time on their hands getting into our business. Are they really trying to help us or just grandstanding and flaunting their self-perceived superiority to make themselves feel better?

Defenders of paternalism have responses. They can reply that, if anything, paternalism is *more* respectful because it merely seeks to correct people's faulty judgment and prevent these shortcomings from getting them into trouble. Such corrections are not attempts to lord over people or run their lives for them. In fact, proper paternalism aims to help people so that they are freer and better able to live their lives as they *themselves* see fit. If Bob cuts his life short by smoking or overeating, or if he fails to save anything for retirement, Bob is diminishing what he can do with his freedom over the course of his life. He will be unable to do as much if he gets cancer or diabetes, or no longer has money to spend on his favorite activities. Bob's quality of life will likely be diminished, but defenders of paternalism can argue that he will *also* be *less* free because his bad decisions bring him harms that reduce the options available to him. By intervening now to prevent Bob from making certain bad choices, we are respecting Bob's future self by preserving his overall freedom. We should respect people in the sense of helping them become better at running their lives. Why should we respect all their bad choices then?

As for paternalism's allegedly insulting nature, Hanna makes the point that there are better and worse ways to intervene. Imagine that you are pulled over for speeding and the police officer berates you and calls you a terrible driver. That's insulting, but it doesn't change the fact that you shouldn't have been speeding. It only shows that the officer could have issued your ticket in a more civil and polite manner. Likewise, a paternalist shouldn't demean your intelligence and worth when she intervenes, but if she does, that only shows that she is being rude, not that the intervention *as such* is wrong. Perhaps certain paternalistic laws and regulations *feel* insulting, but feelings don't necessarily make it so. Such laws and regulations may be frustrating at times when they stop you from doing what you want to do in the moment, but frustration is not the same as being an object of insult, especially if those laws and regulations ultimately serve your best interest.

Paternalism imposes values (or views or reasons) on people: Most of us want to live our lives as we see fit, even if we make mistakes along the way. We would object to others imposing their religious views on us, or their tastes in clothing or cuisine, even if others sincerely (and perhaps *correctly*) thought these different views and tastes would benefit us. We do not merely possess a life – it's *our* lives to decide what to think and believe, and how to act. There's no point in being an agent if someone else gets to make the key decisions and treat us like a puppet on a string. The characters from the dystopian novel *Brave New World* had all their needs provided by the state – they may have lived pleasant lives stoned on soma, but would these be the sorts of lives *you* would prefer? Part of being an individual is having the freedom to think for oneself and have discretion about what to do *even* if someone else knows one's best interests better. Life is about making one's own way and learning from mistakes, right?

Defenders can respond that this objection exaggerates the strength and scope of paternalism. No thoughtful paternalist is arguing that we should *always* intervene in *all* areas of a person's life and dictate what they should do and why they should do it. The best defenses of paternalism go to great lengths in stressing that effective interventions should be infrequent, only directed at significantly risky and harmful choices, and as nonintrusive as possible. Always intervening would defeat the purpose of Hanna's pro-paternalism, for instance, because at some point too many interventions would likely set back a person's overall interests rather than advance them.

Moreover, interventions should be as aligned as possible with the target's own beliefs and values, provided their beliefs are not obviously false and their values not clearly screwed up. Now if someone believes that drinking poison will make her stronger, or she really likes torturing puppies, we can probably step in without much controversy to stop these bad choices. Are we imposing our beliefs and values on her? Perhaps, but if it's not wrong in these cases, why think it wrong in cases where people harm *themselves* through errors in thinking or clearly screwy values? (Liberal democracies are tolerant of differing values, but we have to draw a line at some point, and puppy torture is one of those cases.)

We can even turn the matter on its head. We sometimes impose values in *non*-paternalistic cases like stopping puppy torture, and these cases don't seem objectionable even if we are imposing. Conversely, we may *not* in fact be imposing values when we keep a person from doing to himself what he acknowledges he shouldn't do. So it's unclear whether value imposition is even the issue with paternalism. Limited paternalism is meant to prevent a person from making the kinds of choices which detract from the rest of *that person's* overall interest, all things considered. For instance, Bob stubbornly insists on not wearing a seat belt when he drives. This refusal serves no major benefit in his life (and seat belts don't cause him discomfort or delays) compared to the risks of harm he faces if he gets in an accident.

A paternalist can argue, quite plausibly, that Bob's *own* beliefs and values commit him to the wisdom of buckling up in order to protect the rest of what he values. He has no good reason for his stubborn refusal, and so a law requiring Bob to wear a seat belt for his own good is not imposing any views on him he wouldn't already hold if he had first thought things through. (But I will argue in Chapters 3 and 4 that this imposition objection has teeth – in fact, I think a version of it provides a formidable challenge to paternalism once fleshed out.)

Paternalism violates individual rights: This claim is that people own themselves and so they and only they have the right to decide what they will do, for better or worse. They possess the final word over intimate decisions such as what to do with their own bodies. The paternalist who doesn't allow you to do with yourself what you want is to that extent part-owner of you. But we don't belong to others in liberal democracies. We allow people to have abortions and destroy fine works of art that they own, so how are paternalists permitted to stop us from doing whatever we want to ourselves?

Paternalists can respond that this objector needs to give an *argument* for why such a full self-ownership right exists. Merely asserting a right against paternalism will not do since it begs the question about how such a right is justified in the first place. Even if we do own ourselves in some sense, ownership need not be all or nothing. I own my dog, so I have a certain bundle of powers over her that others lack. Nobody can take her from me without good reason, I can sell or give her away, I can dress her in silly pup sweaters, etc. But I don't have a right to beat her, even despite my legitimate ownership claims. Because she is a sentient being, I may not treat her any old way – I don't own her in the same way I own my trash can. Other widely recognized rights refer to their importance in securing our freedom, equality, and interests – a right to harm oneself doesn't as clearly fall into these categories.

Moreover, if the claim is that paternalism violates one's right not to have one's autonomy infringed, why does this right not apply to cases where one's autonomy is infringed in order to prevent harm to *others*, which nobody denies is sometimes allowed? It seems arbitrary to apply in one case but not the other. I may have the right in general to swing a baseball bat, but I don't have the right to swing it at another person's head. Nobody would object to my right being limited in this way, but how are things all that different if I'm about to swing the bat at my *own* head? I have the right to bash in my own brains but not someone else's? Why? Perhaps I do have such a right, but the point is that this right requires a defense and not merely a table-pounding (head-pounding?) assertion. It's not at all obvious that we have strong rights against paternalism in the same way that we have rights not to be assaulted or defrauded.

Paternalism is likely to be misapplied or abused: Proponents of the misapplication concern often cite slippery slopes typically toward more and more coercive laws. Take the example of seat belt laws. Originally, most cars did not come with seat belts, but as concerns about safety grew, laws began requiring manufacturers to include seat belts though drivers were not required to wear them. Then later laws began requiring drivers but not backseat passengers to wear them. Then finally laws required everyone in the car to wear seat belts.

Anti-smoking laws are another example. Originally people could smoke pretty much wherever they wanted. Then smoking was banned in many public places because of concerns about harm to others who had no other way of avoiding secondhand smoke. But for a long time, private businesses could still permit smoking since it was the owner's property. Then many cities began passing ordinances banning smoking in clubs and restaurants because of secondhand smoke concerns for employees and customers. Now there is some talk about banning smoking in private residences, if not banning tobacco cigarettes altogether. Here the justification has slid from harm to others to protecting the smoker's own well-being.

The main concern reflected by the slippery slope argument is that once a law, however moderate, is put into place, its precedent plants the seed for more and more restrictive laws. With paternalism, even if a proposed regulation isn't very objectionable on its own terms, its very enforcement sets the stage for more and more intrusive paternalism, especially when the people who propose the laws are not the same as those tasked with enforcing them, often years and decades later.[10]

Proponents of the abuse concern reflect a view sometimes called "public choice economics". This view maintains that people in the public and political sphere tend to have the same motivations that they have in private and market spheres. They don't magically become more public-spirited once in power, and in fact they might become more liable to shenanigans. Politicians, policymakers, bureaucrats, and even many voters are not always acting from adequate information and concern for the common good. Politicians are trying to get elected and stay elected, so they might be tempted to appeal to rhetoric that inflames the passions of uninformed voters rather than appeal to facts. They might exaggerate the threat of crime or the dangers of smoking. (Many Americans believe the U.S. is more violent now than ever, even though rates of violent crime have fallen steadily since the early 90s.)

Bureaucrats often look to increase the budget of their agency, so they might be tempted to exaggerate some alleged threat (like recreational drug use or terrorism) and claim that we need their resources to fight it (think the Drug Enforcement Agency or the Transportation Security Administration). In fact, failure to achieve an agency's goals is often used as a reason to *increase* that agency's budget, on the grounds that failure was simply due to lack of sufficient resources and not because the agency's goals were unrealistic. The idea is basically that even well-meaning people who pass and enforce laws are themselves often acting from limited information and sometimes self-serving motives. We can't assume that a given law or regulation, even if it's a good idea in theory, won't turn out to be used as an excuse to pass further unnecessary and even counterproductive measures.

Defenders of paternalistic laws need not deny that such laws may be subject to slippery slopes or abuse, but they can say this is a concern for *all* legislation handled by flawed humanity. It's not a *distinctive* problem for paternalism. If one argues that we shouldn't have legislation on the chance that such laws would be misapplied or abused, then one is arguing that we shouldn't have any legislation at all! Maybe this is a fine result if you are a hard-nosed anarchist who thinks there shouldn't be a state, but most people don't share that view and you'll have a lot of work on your hands trying to convince them otherwise. Still, if it turned out that paternalistic laws tended to do more harm than good, this would just mean that such laws are not feasible to pass or enforce, not that paternalism is morally wrong as such. It would still not be rationally or perhaps morally OK to make certain bad choices, but the law at least, if not private actors, shouldn't do anything to stop them. So in a different sense, it would at least be *legally* OK to make such bad choices.

Maybe paternalism isn't as bad as its detractors make it out to be. Still, you might be wondering why we ever need to use coercion on competent adults if instead we can use persuasion and efforts to educate them. The less intrusive the intervention, the better, right? This might be the case if we had good evidence that education is often effective, but some defenders of paternalism are skeptical. Sarah Conly, a defender of paternalism, writes: "Educating people simply isn't all that effective, because in some areas we are relatively ineducable."[11] She uses smoking as an example. We have known for decades that smoking carries many health risks, but we still see lots of people doing it. The percentage of new smokers has declined, sure, but something like 20% of the U.S. population still lights up. The message gets through to some but not to significant numbers of people whom we might think should know better. Why is this? Let us now turn to Conly's discussion of why education about risks is often not effective and so coercive paternalism may sometimes be in order.

CONLY'S DEFENSE OF LEGAL PATERNALISM

Conly defends a version of paternalism that focuses on the ways in which people's cognitive shortcomings often obstruct where they want to go with their own goals. As discussed previously, we commonly have failures of rationality. We want to lose weight but then remain stuck to the couch and mindlessly indulging in Funyuns. We want to save more for retirement but often put off setting up a savings account when all we have to do is fill out a form at work. We want to quit smoking but give in to wishful thinking and procrastination, never considering that each cigarette we smoke adds up over time and may make us very ill one day. It is not hard to find many instances in which we often fail to live up to our own goals because we act in ways that conflict with good steps toward those goals, and we do so not out of carefully thought-out choice but because of carelessness, laziness, stubbornness, or self-deception.

Conly claims to be largely neutral about what people's goals are and is more concerned with paternalism's role in correcting the choices they make that obstruct reaching those goals. Her approach holds that certain activities are just things that no *educated* person would start doing if they sufficiently appreciated the costs relative to the rest of what they valued. Her concern is not about people's preferences over what goals to have, which she regards as fairly stable. Rather, her concern is about people's preferences over how to reach those goals, preferences which can be misinformed or downright conflicting.

Moreover, Conly recognizes that there is a variety of conceptions of the good: "Even if it makes conceptual sense to speak of one particular kind of life as being objectively better than another . . . it is clearly controversial what that objectively better life consists in."[12] She's not looking to impose her favorite view on us. Like Hanna, Conly's initial strategy is to claim that most people accept mild paternalism like prescriptions and seat belt laws, but they don't then give good arguments for why the line should be drawn there and not extended to other harmful actions such as smoking or soda over-consumption.[13]

Let us consider three arguments. First, Conly confronts standard critiques of paternalism like those discussed previously, the first being that it is disrespectful because it treats adults like helpless children. She attempts to invert this claim: "respect becomes a justification for inhumanity: the principle that those who fail deserve to fail isn't one that is geared to support equality and mutual respect."[14] Imagine an antipaternalist "utopia", a world in which uneducated people are free to shoot up heroin, drive unbelted, eat lots of sugar, and not save enough for retirement. It may be easy for an opponent of paternalism to say they respected the freedom of people to make bad choices, knowing fully well that many of these people would proceed to abuse their freedom of choice.

That easy "tolerance" goes nowhere, however, when people subsequently suffer from overdoses, brain trauma or death, diabetes or obesity, and poverty in old age. "You made your bed – now lie in it" or "serves you right" or "you belong in the gutter" are not then attitudes reflecting respect. Instead they are cruel reminders of allowing freedoms that perhaps we are not fit to have as flawed beings. If anything, such attitudes reflect an elitist scorn that antipaternalists often accuse paternalists of having. The irony of claiming that antipaternalism shows more respect is strengthened if we look at the freedoms, such as the ability to drink large sodas, which antipaternalists apparently regard as symbols of dignity.[15] How is a Big Gulp a sign of freedom's inherent value? (Perhaps a few true-blue libertarian characters, such as Ron Swanson from the show *Parks and Recreation*, would celebrate such freedoms as the real American way, but most of us aren't like Ron . . . are we?)

Here antipaternalists claim to respect vulnerable people by honoring their alleged right to engage in fairly trivial freedoms that risk severe harm, or leave them responsible for important choices that make them vulnerable, and then fail to provide relief or even compassion on the occasions people suffer the ill effects of acting on those freedoms and responsibilities. A society composed of one group of people suffering from these bad consequences, even if the consequences were to some degree those people's own fault, is not one consistent with equality and respect for human dignity. A poorly educated underclass facing health problems, disability, or impoverishment whatever the source of these ills is not a group poised to realize fair terms of cooperation with better-off citizens. If anything, respect requires that we all agree to restrict our freedoms in some ways so as to better reach our goals and sometimes even better protect our overall freedom.

In fact, Conly emphasizes that paternalism is democratic and not about one group of elites restricting the freedom of underlings. Rather, it's *all* of us at our best agreeing to restrict *all* of us at our worst. That is, we (including paternalists like Conly herself!) are all equally subject to paternalistic laws because we are all vulnerable to potential lapses in the quality of our decisions. Nothing about such laws implies disrespect and certainly not inequality. Big Brother treating us like little children under His watchful, caring, but authoritarian gaze is a myth about serious defenses of paternalism. Allowing people the freedom to make very bad decisions, on the other hand, can result in situations where precisely such inequality or disrespect runs wild.

Conly's first point can be firmed up by the fact that we are not merely subject to weakness of will. Our mistakes are not always just owing to stubbornness, laziness, or other failures of effort. According to her, defenders of absolute and total free choice often maintain that "the ground for valuing liberty is the claim that we are pre-eminently rational agents, each of us well suited to determining what goes on in our own life." We are not such agents, however, so "we should save people from doing things that are gravely bad for them when they do that *only* as a result of an error in thinking."[16] We should intervene to save people rather than merely try to persuade or inform them because "sometimes no amount of public education can get someone to realize, in a sufficiently vivid sense, the potential dangers of his course of behavior. If public education were effective, we would have no new smokers, but we do."[17] Thoughtful paternalists would be happy to live in a world where persuasion, informational campaigns, and gentle nudges were all we needed to keep people from acting against their best interests. But plainly such interventions don't always succeed, so we need coercion.

Second, Conly makes clear that her defense of legal paternalism is not meant to extend to all or even most of our actions:

> Legislation should intervene when people are likely to make decisions that seriously and irrevocably interfere with their ability to reach their goals, and where legislation can reliably prevent them from making those bad decisions, and where legislation is the least costly thing that can reliably prevent them from making those bad decisions. The majority of decisions we make do not meet these conditions.[18]

Conly admits that she has no principled objection to a much wider scope for paternalistic laws than she thinks is possible in our world, but any realistic legislation must be practical, accounting for costs and not merely focusing on possible benefits.

The "nanny state" imagined by some critics of paternalism is not something serious defenders advocate. Not only would such a state be terribly expensive in monetary terms, we would be chilled by a state that had extensive access to information about our private lives. We'd be annoyed by an army of enforcers always ready to crack down whenever they deemed that we should not have that donut. There is a big difference between a ban on trans fats and cigarettes, which most of us would not miss, and a ban on ice cream sundaes or rock music. There is a big difference between a "1984"-style dystopia where Big Brother spies on us in our houses and forces us to exercise, and a helpful mandate that one save for retirement or purchase health insurance.

Third, Conly argues that most of us *want* paternalism to protect us from making some potentially bad choices:

> While some people write as if every time a freedom were taken from us we kick and scream and feel deprived, others, more realistic, recognize that the responsibility for making such choices is a burden, and one that we are often quite willing to give up.[19]

Navigating difficult financial decisions, or having the responsibility to research whether the food we eat is nutritious or full of junk, is simply something we may lack the time, energy, or ability to do. Moreover, the belief that we should be free and responsible to make these kinds of choices suggests that we have more control over some of our situations than we really do.

Paternalism can help rid us of the illusion that we are more rational and prudent than we really are: "Reality checks don't close off options, although they sometimes may reveal that we don't have options we mistakenly thought we had. This, of course, helps us recognize our true options."[20] Naturally existing costs, needs, and competition all constrain and provide roadblocks to our decisions, good or bad. They get in the way of what we might want to do in a given moment, though we don't regard these as unacceptable but as part of life, so it is unclear why we should blame paternalistic laws for providing roadblocks only to some of our *worst* decisions.

Our goals are often frustrated by obstacles we accept as a part of life. Far from being a major obstacle to our true goals, effective paternalism can help us avoid such barriers as getting in our own way: "Life is structured around the negotiation of obstacles, of which paternalistic laws are typically the slightest."[21] When unfulfilling but daily decisions "are also difficult, requiring expertise, and important, such that a failure in their regard can substantially alter our quality of life, it can be liberating to have them taken out of our hands."[22] Just before that passage she writes: "There are, probably, an infinite number of ways in which we can use our powers of discrimination, and for most of us, some are simply not that fulfilling." Paternalism still allows many opportunities to use these powers in ways one sees fit, without one falling prey to severely harmful decisions. Despite the title of her book being *Against Autonomy*, Conly takes pains to emphasize how there are many ways to live one's own life – and perhaps live it better and freer – under legal paternalism.

There is also a distinction between the quality and importance of the various types of choices that might confront us. Conly argues, for instance, that we don't restrict pursuit of relationships because "we really enjoy the process, even if the outcome is a failure."[23] At least for some cultures, the pursuit of romantic relationships is a large part of their value: courtship rituals, honeymoon periods, seduction, learning to compromise out of love, etc. Yes, relationships can fail miserably, but recall the earlier discussion about how, while a failed marriage can be a severe harm, it is not usually immediate or irreversible. The freedom to fail at marriage matters more because forming or maintaining relationships "makes up a large part of the narrative of our lives."

Thoughtful paternalists more generally "want to respect your ends, rather than impose what they may think of as more sensible ones upon you."[24] But mundane areas of choice – such as buckling up or deciding whether to eat foods containing

Why It's OK to Make Bad Choices

lots of sugar or trans fats – can be rightly subject to external interference and that should not bother us since they don't make up a large part of the narrative of our lives. Others can do the legwork and we can enjoy eating without the tiresome business of learning about and making proper decisions to avoid the obviously bad stuff. There seems little objectionable about outsourcing an unpleasant or boring task to someone with the knowledge and motivation to take up that burden, and if our democratic institutions are up to the job, it is permissible for them to go forward regardless of our individual consent to each and every law.

BUT . . .

So let's fly the flag of paternalism, right? Not so fast. I have a few cards up my sleeve, or so I think. As a reminder: in the next chapter I will discuss some ways in which it is often quite difficult for us (especially anyone other than perhaps close friends or family) to know whether in fact a person is acting in her own interest when she makes what appears to us to be bad choices. If we are unsure, however, then we can't always assume that they are making genuinely bad choices that might call for paternalism, whether legal or private. This consideration raises problems for Conly but perhaps not for Hanna. In Chapter 3 I will discuss how it might not be OK *as such* for us to make genuinely bad choices, but it might nonetheless be OK to have the *freedom* to make such choices even when acknowledge the choices are bad. Chapter 4 will discuss why we run the risk of imposing our views on others if we assume that they must first be committed to this freedom to make bad choices in order to be exempt from paternalistic laws. Chapter 5 looks at whether most of our bad choices are sufficiently out of our control that we need *soft* paternalism in many cases. Our choices may be bad in these cases largely because they aren't really ours. Chapter 6 will be a break from the paternalism discussion! There I will discuss whether it might not be OK to make bad choices if they impose undue costs on others who did not agree to these costs. So maybe the main reason it's bad to eat junk food is not so much because I harm myself, but because I end up imposing costs on you for my health care. Chapter 7 will argue that, even if you aren't persuaded by my case, we might still need to be careful, especially when making hard paternalism a matter of *legal*, not merely occasional *private*, coercion.[25] Restricting many bad choices could make matters worse than merely allowing such choices.

I hope you have enjoyed the ride so far, reader, and I hope to have laid out a strong enough initial case for legal paternalism that you find it plausible or even convincing. Now buckle up (if you choose) because I'm about to try to convince you why paternalistic laws and policies are typically unjustified to those who don't already want such for themselves.

Two

I ate a donut this morning. Mmm – it was good (thanks for asking). More precisely, I made the choice to eat a donut rather than something else, when I had other options, including healthier fare such as an apple or a whole-grain bagel. So why did I decide to eat a donut?

There are many possible reasons . . . I like the taste, the smell, or the texture. It goes well with coffee. I was walking by the shop and it seemed like a nice change – you know, from my normal apple and whole-grain bagel. I was rewarding myself for finishing writing a book chapter the night before. I ran into an old friend who offered to buy me a donut and, despite being utterly satisfied by the apple and whole-grain bagel I had eaten earlier, I accepted this offer out of my natural impulse to be friendly and sociable. Or the stunning woman with the wonderfully green eyes and dazzlingly charming smile behind the counter made the donut sound like heaven. . . .

I chose to eat that donut because it served my interests to do so – my true interests, which are complex and multifaceted, and include desires, goals, principles, and much more. I may have eaten that donut for any of the reasons I listed, for countless other reasons that I didn't list, or any combination of these. I may not have been aware, even, of the reason I ate that donut but it was the choice I made. Was it the best choice I could have made, or even a good one? I could certainly ask myself that question, but to answer it I would have to know my own interests. It may have been a terrible decision, but that's for me – and only me – to assess.[1]

These opening remarks from Mark D. White's book critical of paternalism are worth quoting because they capture the spirit of what I will explore in this chapter: people are very complicated no matter how well or poorly their lives are going. Of course, they do not *always*, in every instance, know their own good best – as discussed in Chapter 1 – but they are ultimately the ones running their lives and most familiar with all the intricate details of their situations at a given moment. At least, we face heavy constraints in determining whether a person who seems to be making bad choices is really doing so. We don't often know what's going on in their minds. As the comic book writer Harvey Pekar said, "Ordinary life is pretty complex stuff."

Here's the thing – most contemporary defenders of paternalism *agree* that welfare is subjective. That is, there isn't some Objective and True Good Out There that we should all pursue in order to live a good life. Instead, a good life is judged by the goals we set and the preferences we have with regard to pursuing those goals. This subjective view of welfare doesn't at all mean that anything goes . . . far from it. The view stresses, in fact, that people can have inconsistent preferences that undermine their goals. For instance, one goal I might have is to live a long and healthy life where I get to see my grandkids flourish, but if I also like smoking and eating trans-fatty foods, I could very well be undermining that goal. Paternalism aimed at stopping my unhealthy habits could better position me to accomplish the goals I want to see happen if I had access to the relevant information.

However, a challenge for paternalists is how to identify what people's preferences are such that they can make a confident assessment of when paternalism is warranted. *I will argue that their commitment to subjectivism about goods should in fact tilt them away* from *paternalism*. In this chapter, I will introduce a cast of characters to join White's donut eater. In the remainder of this chapter, I will explore some ways in which it's not at all clear that people are making actually bad choices – even by their own lights – when they do things some of us tend not to like. If their choices are merely "bad", but not actually bad on subjective grounds, then maybe they should be free to make them.

Let's meet our four characters. I am going to assign them a somewhat artificial score on a scale of 0–100, worst-to-best, based on how well their lives are going. How did I come up with this scale? There's no science behind it. It's really more of a way to compare people's lives against each other. If there is some objective way of scoring a life – I'm not sure that's possible, but let's roll with it for now – then the scores are only meant as rough ways to capture how good a person's life has been on average until now. Think of it as your average bowling score or however many points you average in your favorite Xbox game . . . but for a life. Now here's our cast:

Badly-off Bob (5 of 100): 5 so far, but that 5 probably isn't going up. Bob lives in a rural and remote town. The technical term for this place is a "dump". The main industry in his town shut down long ago and there is widespread unemployment. When he can find it, Bob works odd jobs to try to make ends meet so he can afford the low rent on his squalid shack infested with rats and raccoons. He tries to chase them off but they always return. Why doesn't he just move then? How? He can barely scrape by day-to-day. The nearest supermarket is 20 miles away, his 1982 Buick Skylark barely works anymore, and so Bob's meals mainly come from the nearby gas station he walks to. They are typically hot dogs and taquitos. On fancy nights he gets a slice of pizza and washes it down with some malt liquor. He smokes one–two packs a day and uses meth regularly because it sometimes makes him feel euphoric and powerful. His teeth are rotting and he may have tapeworms. Is Bob making bad choices? Different question: Is he making bad choices *given the options available to him?*

Well-off Wynn (90 of 100): Wynn is crushing it at life, so much so that her friends have nicknamed her "Wynner". She has an exciting and lucrative job as a venture capitalist in uptown Manhattan that lets her travel around the world. She's in her mid-30s and has been working almost non-stop since college to get to where she is. What she's missing is a solid and lasting relationship. She has friends and casual lovers but she's ready to settle down. However, her job keeps her very busy and she has limited opportunities to find suitable dating partners. She smokes three packs a week and finds that groups on a smoking break are a good way to meet people outside the office. She also finds that this subculture of smokers tends to be more up her alley in terms of interests and personalities. They tend to be more laid-back and adventurous, with similar tastes in art and music. She is well aware of smoking's health risks, but she is hoping that treatments for smoking-related ailments will be abundant in 30 years. She is in good health, and there is no genetic predisposition toward cancer in her family, but if there were, she might consider quitting sooner rather than later. Anyway, is she making bad choices given her circumstances? Should we force her not to smoke?

Football Fred (80 of 100): 80 so far, and maybe it will hold steady while he has lots of food and finally hangs out with his family regularly, hosting cookouts, eating junk food, guzzling down sugary sodas, and binge-watching HBO and Netflix series after retiring from football. For most of his life so far, he ate healthy but not always flavorful food, got up at 5 a.m. to train for hours, and exhausted himself many times on

Sunday trying to win the game while armchair coaches criticized him for never winning a championship despite his Hall of Fame statistics. Fred now gets to sit back and enjoy things on his own terms – without sports reporters and fans constantly on his case. He loses his magnificent physique after retirement and gains 100 pounds in a few years, but he has never felt happier even if he isn't accomplishing rare athletic feats anymore. That doesn't matter to him now because it was a different time in his life and he's more than happy to move on. He will probably get diabetes in his 50s. partly based on family history, partly based on his diet. Is he making bad choices? Should we tax or ban the unhealthy food he enjoys?

Physicist Phil (98 of 100): Phil has led a fantastic and successful life. He won the Nobel Prize in physics after solving the most perplexing and deepest problems of his time. He's gone on the lecture circuit, his books are now bestsellers, and he is famous around the world. He has no partner or kids because he spent so much of his time grappling with the mysteries of the universe. He's approaching his 60s and doesn't really find the prospect of trying to start a family all that plausible. Phil is quite happy looking back on how well things went, but he knows that things aren't going to go as well from now on. He's had it so good that he wants to kill himself with an overdose of painkillers and a bottle of 40-year-old scotch that an old flame once gave him for his birthday. "Why in the world would he do such a thing?" we gasp in unison. He wants to end his life while on top instead of declining into what he sees as a dull anticlimax without anything like the thrills of discovery he had the fortune to experience. He doesn't care about living out his biological life span especially if he has nowhere to go but down. The NFL quarterback John Elway retired on top after winning two championships in his final two seasons.

Michael Jordan retired twice after winning three straight NBA championships both times. You might say "well, that's sports, but we're talking about a life here." Maybe so, but if retiring on top makes sense in the limited context of a career, is it all that insane when applied to the entirety of one's life? Is Phil making a bad (nay, terrible) choice to end his life peacefully and painlessly? Should we stop him, or revive him against his will if we happen across his unconscious body and read his suicide note?

Maybe someone beyond oneself would lead one never to entertain such an option as Phil's suicide. Still, because of personality or circumstances, not everyone has deep social connections, so it isn't obvious that paternalism is called for even in some of the more extreme examples like Phil's story. But if we are hesitant to prevent people from harming themselves in the previous examples, are there perhaps not millions of other people who harm themselves for particular reasons that we cannot necessarily understand simply by looking through the lens of general values like health and wealth? Perhaps defenders of paternalism can tell us why paternalism might still be in line for some of these people. Despite Wynn's talent, perhaps she is uneducated and ignorant with regard to smoking. Despite Phil's genius at science, perhaps he is ignorant about how dire his decision to commit suicide really is. After all, his life can still be meaningful even if all the extraordinary parts are over.

A CRITIQUE OF CONLY

While Sarah Conly is right that critics of paternalism too frequently claim their view is most consistent with respect while not adequately defending this claim, antipaternalists need not hold to a particular view about attitudes or actions we should have toward those who have made bad choices. It may be tragic that someone chose poorly and suffered bad consequences because of that choice, but whether we hold that person blameworthy, or not deserving of aid, is a separate matter (see Chapter 6 on the aid issue). Whether we continue to respect this person's dignity regardless of the bad decisions he has made is also a separate matter. One would assume that we continue to respect his dignity no matter what, because he is still a person capable of choosing, etc.

Either way, focusing on sodas as the symbols of dignity is an unusual move since it is the choosing person who has dignity, not her particular choices to overindulge. And perhaps her decision *not* to overindulge, when she could have done so, may lend her yet more dignity. Avoidance of bad decisions – when one was free *not* to avoid these things – is part of what I will argue (in Chapter 3) gives a great deal of dignity to persons capable of choice. Freedom and dignity need not at all be symbolized by what some would deride as shallow and mindless consumerism, but instead symbolized as providing the opportunity for making good choices when one could have made bad ones.

Moreover, Conly assumes that plausible objections to paternalism suppose that we are these super smart beings who automatically choose correctly, but that is not the only grounds for objecting. The myth of the perfectly rational agent is not something required for arguments against paternalism. Our rationality is limited, and it's quite clear that we mess up sometimes, but we are still capable of acting more or less rationally within those limits. One key question is whether some error is innocent (like in Mill's bridge example) or whether the agent should have known better than to commit it and could have avoided committing it without undue effort. When people make seemingly bad choices, is it because they are (1) incapable of being educated, (2) unwilling to be educated, or (3) indeed educated but want to make the "bad" choice anyway? These various explanations could have different bearings on the question of whether we should make a person stop acting in some way.

If (1) is the case, then Mill's bridge example and soft paternalism seem to be in play – a person incapable of learning about the dangers of some action may then not even know what they're doing. We *presume* they don't want this because we don't have the opportunity to elicit their preferences before they act. If (2) is the case, then a person might just be too lazy or stubborn to listen when they should know better, but that's a different story because they are being willingly ignorant, not innocently so, and hard paternalism is in play.

If (3) is the case, then a person is knowingly assuming the risks. The question of whether we are ineducable then depends on the reasons for which we may persist in performing seemingly foolish actions despite exposure to information and persuasion. We outside observers face our own informational constraints, however, as there may be no objective way "to distinguish between (a) customers who absorbed the relevant information and decided rationally to assume the risks and (b) customers who did not hear a compelling enough narrative about the risk."[2]

Conly claims that there would be no new smokers if sufficient education about its ills were effective. This is not obvious – recall Badly-off Bob and Well-off Wynn. The question-begging conclusion is that since people still take up smoking, they must not have had sufficient access to the decisive reasons not to smoke, rather than making an informed decision to assume the risks anyway. This conclusion moves too quickly since a key question here – one not obvious to us outsiders – is whether someone is in control of their ability to become more informed, or, being sufficiently informed, decides to assume a risk anyway, given that risk's place in their lives. If so, that may be all we need to know about them. But there may be no way of knowing whether someone who appreciated the potential health hazards of smoking, who could vividly imagine what lung cancer or emphysema involved, would in fact decide against smoking in light of that appreciation.

We could as easily assume that someone confronted with warnings might nonetheless find the risks worth it, especially if their life situation makes those risks worth it (Bob), or if they're buying time in anticipation of medical advances that may cure the diseases caused by smoking (Wynn). There may be no testable way to ascertain whether a person "gets it" but decides to smoke anyway. There may be no good way, short of hearing a smoker rehearse the health hazards of smoking, for determining whether they got the message but nevertheless decided to take the risk. Even then, we can't be sure whether their rehearsal reflects a sincere appraisal or is cheap talk for fear of otherwise facing contemporary disapproval of smoking.

I mentioned in Chapter 1 how some people might take up smoking out of pressure to conform among their peer group, but it goes both ways – some smokers might lie that they want to quit out of feeling a similar pressure! If Conly's defense of paternalism rests on helping people get to where they want to go, then we should by and large trust their self-reports about where they want to go and how they decide to try getting there. They may even try paying for quitting devices, which is strong but not decisive evidence of their wanting to quit. Why not decisive? They could be under pressure from others to quit and hence pay for the devices, or they might be wondering whether they can quit but decide after the devices fail that they must really like smoking. Regardless, we can never be sure whether in fact the person before us really wants to smoke despite its risks, but then we can never be sure whether in fact the person wants to quit either. At some point, self-reports are a matter of disclosure which each of us is responsible for conveying, right?

Conly's passage explaining the limits of paternalistic legislation is ambiguous between whether people are (1) likely to make risky decisions, but ones that don't typically result in severe and irreversible harm that undermines their goals, or (2) likely to make risky decisions that will likely result in severe and irreversible harm that undermines their goals. This distinction is important. If she means (2), that seems to conflict with the fact that most people in liberal democracies today live fairly long lives *even when* left to decide whether to undertake behavior that Conly thinks should be banned. Would paternalism help many of them to a significant degree? It's not at all clear. They might not reach all their goals, if reaching end-of-life goals is what matters most, but that often owes itself to circumstances or choices that have little to do with falling victim to severe and irreversible harm. People come up short all the time for various reasons: their goals were too ambitious, they didn't work hard enough, there were setbacks beyond their control, etc.

If she means (1), then it's unclear what the odds are of risky decisions resulting in the level of harms she claims warrants intervention. Most risky decisions do not lead to severe and irreversible harms and allow people enough time to learn from feedback. Indeed, most of the bad decisions she finds apt targets of paternalism (smoking, failure to save, overspending, failure to wear seat belts or helmets, poor dietary habits, gambling, addiction, running up debts) are not one-off decisions that pose severe and immediate risks of tragedy. Procrastinating on some important matter is not the same as whimsically jumping off a cliff. So what are the goals people have such that the usual suspects severely compromise pursuit of those goals? Opponents of paternalism can take Conly at her word that she endorses quite limited legislation that leaves people free to run most aspects of their lives. Nonetheless, few choices at any time need be as bad as she claims, so maybe there is very little scope for legal paternalism by her own premises.

Why Be Ideally Rational?

Despite widespread commitment to subjectivity and its respect for individual preferences, paternalists often employ a demanding standard to model what preferences an ideally rational agent would have in contrast with the preferences of actual agents. They tend to use a model of the agent with "full attention, complete information, unlimited cognitive abilities, and complete self-control."[3] That's a pretty idealized model that threatens to lose the subjective nature of what they claim to respect. If our preferences differ from that of the ideal agent, it's our preferences that are called into question. Do you know anyone with this heroic combination of information, intelligence, and self-discipline? Paternalists would likely reply that of course nobody is really this godlike. But then it's unclear why this model should be the yardstick for measuring what we flesh-and-blood creatures should do. We are not gods – and that's OK.

When they formalized the axioms of rational choice theory, economists like Kenneth Arrow and Gerard Debreu originally took those axioms simply to be what it *means* to be rational in the sense needed to make the math work. They formulated the basic rules of the theory so they were able to make social scientific predictions of aggregate behavior, not necessarily the behavior of any one individual. Whether anyone *ought* to be rational in this sense is a further matter needing argument.[4] However, some paternalists share the view that this model should also guide our choices. They claim that since we fall short of this ideal, we might need coercion to bring us closer into alignment with this picture of rationality.[5]

Other authors are skeptical, however, that such a standard can even yield predictable behavior. Robert Sugden asks:

> How, without making normative judgments, do we determine what counts as complete information, unlimited cognition, or complete willpower? Even if we can specify what it would mean to have these supernatural powers, how do we discover how some ordinary human being would act if he were somehow to acquire them?[6]

Indeed, we would have to make a bunch of (likely controversial) assumptions. Complete information would need to include all the relevant considerations that might count in favor of some matter, but it is difficult for us to gauge all that is relevant without knowing the biography of the agent for whom some consideration may or may not be relevant. How, for instance, would Bob's biography figure into this description of rationality?

The same goes with unlimited cognition, since it is not clear what conclusions infinite brain powers would yield when ordinary agents like us must make many judgments under uncertainty, when sometimes we don't even know what we don't know. So then how can we know that the judgments of godlike beings would even be *intelligible* to us, let alone attractive, given our limited perspectives? Let's say these supergeniuses discover that the best life ever is to eat oatmeal while wearing a gorilla suit. Our response will likely be ". . ." At first, we'd probably think they're trolling us. But let's say they're perfectly moral and they're correct about this! Even so, how do *we* know they're correct, and how much value would we find in wearing gorilla suits while eating oatmeal?

Complete attention and errorless self-control suggest that agents would automatically choose the right thing, whether in thinking or acting, because they could *never* choose to give in to temptation or neglect to consider what might need considering. But these sound like robots rather than us, who have the freedom of choice to fail at thinking and acting in the proper way. Besides, what fun would life be if we always had no choice but to do the right thing? If we were always successful, effortlessly or not? Wouldn't things get boring fast?

The ideal standard assumes it is something we should all be striving for, but we have limited cognitive resources, and while most everyone wants to be healthier and wealthier if all else were equal . . . all else is typically not equal. Pursuit of these values may require sacrifices of other values people might prefer to pursue in ways the rationality ideal does not capture. For instance, I could probably put in a lot of time and effort trying to decipher the best possible friends, music, or philosophy – but I'm bound by time, place, and circumstances. There are probably lots of errors in my philosophy, and when I notice something is off in my belief system, it might be wise for me to investigate. But that doesn't mean I can question all my beliefs at once.

Odds are, I could like different kinds of music more than what I currently like, but I'm happy with my rock/pop/indie YouTube channels. Chances are that the people I've happened to befriend in my life aren't as compatible as some other people out there whom I'll never meet. Should I leave my current friends and search for new, "better" ones? No way. Part of the value of my narrative is the very "particularity" of it. These are my friends, my music, my philosophy. I wouldn't have it another way because this is the special path my life has taken, and the particular experiences I've encountered are what make me and my situation unique. I belong to this community and not some other, and we have a shared background and experiences that can't merely be substituted by some new and "better" background and experiences. We are partly rooted in the world around us because we are not isolated atoms looking merely to maximize our well-being. We are social beings. But it's not clear that our "ideally rational" robot would see things in this way.

Suppose we could somehow find out these ideal preferences. Still, we have to consider the costs of pursuing their satisfaction from the target's standpoint. Perhaps education and training can make us less inclined to biases, though Thaler and Sunstein acknowledge (indeed insist) it is impossible to debias individuals completely through such avenues.[7] Recall that Conly agrees we are not good at getting educated to avoid bad choices. That being noted, we should compare the benefits of moving closer to the ideal with the costs of intervention, or engaging in efforts at self-correction, if we can only hope to move somewhat closer to perfect rationality.

For instance, the average person might fail to save a certain amount of money by not changing credit cards, but for this failure to be overall costly to her, the benefits she doesn't get must outweigh the costs of searching for and acting on this information, or the costs of regulations intended to relieve people of these costs.[8] Jess might save $200 a year by switching cards, but whether she should depends on whether the time and energy it takes for her to find this out – and the other things she could be doing instead of wading through the fine print of credit card policies – is worth less to her than $200. And how does she know *even that*, typically since we don't price out our time with any precision? One need not want to be a bit closer to the otherwise unattainable if the costs meant moving one farther away from the actual preferences with which one identifies.

Despite wide commitment to subjectivism, considerations like health, wealth, or happiness often serve as anchors in discussions by defenders of paternalism. That is, the discussions tend to fasten on these values in the abstract, to the neglect of other values that might be traded off against health, etc. This neglect often prevents one from considering more nuanced matters about how such values show up in another person's conception of the good, given her situation as a whole. Badly-off Bob might want to be healthier, but he also wants to be high as an escape from his current woeful state of affairs. He can't have both so he chooses to be high. For some, an autonomous life may not be as happy or healthy as a coerced life, but maybe it's a more *important* life for whatever set of reasons (I will explore some of these reasons in Chapter 3).

An external party's predictions often can't track the target's other values and their weights. This need not even involve Conly's observation of how people often take improper steps to their own goals when they act self-harmfully. Although certain activities compromise goals someone finds important, it doesn't follow that those activities lack value for him. Perhaps they vary in strength of value depending on how interested an artist is in a chance at greatness or her confidence in attaining it in her lifetime. She *does* want to make great art if she can, but maybe she *also* wants to have a really fun time even if it cuts her life short. Denying that a person always best knows how to attain her own good does not commit one to denying that a person is the judge of her ultimate goals and how they fit into her life narrative. We are generally not as well-placed as she is in identifying how her interests fit together.

Let us assume nobody really wants to be obese. That seems fair enough. Nonetheless, I challenge the claim that many people are *irrational* to eat enough to make themselves obese and thus tend to have shorter life spans with attendant maladies. Some really enjoy eating and are willing to face the attendant trade-off. Sure, they'd prefer to eat a lot *and* stay at a normal weight, but, being somewhat rational, they know they can't have both and so choose food over having fit and healthy bodies. Are all of these people making these choices because of biases or weak will or bad information? That seems doubtful, since we typically have to make trade-offs between competing values in all walks of life. (Assuming monogamy, should Rachel date Ross or Joey? Should I work on editing this chapter or work on tweaking my Dungeons and Dragons character?)

Enjoying food a lot, or for sentimental reasons, versus staying healthy is one such trade-off. Some people choose to eat less and be healthier, but that doesn't mean it's the true and correct trade-off for every person to make. Of course, maybe some people want to lose weight and are struggling with overeating, but how do *we* outsiders reliably know which folks are these? Others could overeat as a response to stressors, which may well be a rational response to a difficult situation if healthier or more attractive options are not easily available.

Consider the situation of many poor people. They may live in remote rural or blighted urban areas and lack adequate access to affordable nutritious food. Many of the worse-off also lack meaningful work and suffer from troubled relationships. They may not be in as bad a shape as Badly-off Bob, but they still lack much hope for a better future. For many of them, that pack of menthols, or triple cheeseburger with fries and a giant soda, may be what gets them through days in which there seems little else to look forward to.

Instead of taking away something that gets them through those days, perhaps we should first see if we can improve their lives and then see whether they respond by making healthier choices. If so, cool, let's help them improve and allow them some hope. If there isn't much we can do for them, unfortunately, then maybe the worst-off should have *more* freedom from paternalism than the better-off since they have much less to lose! (Maybe write a paper or op-ed on this whether you agree or disagree.) When we see impoverished Bob take meth and assume that he's stupidly making a bad choice *especially because* he's poor, we should remember that maybe Bob (accurately?) feels like there isn't much else he can do with his day. He doesn't have a Prius he can drive to a nearby Whole Foods and buy arugula after a productive day at the office. His job, if he has one, may be menial with little prospect of growth. He may lack any meaningful relationships with family or friends – perhaps his meth buddies are all he has for social connections.

Paternalists who defend subjectivism are right to do so. My main point is that we often lack adequate information about each person's specific circumstances and unique reasons for how they respond to those situations. Simply labeling them ignorant or uneducated in light of these choices is too hasty.

(Remember that old saying about not judging a person until you walk a mile in their shoes.) We rush to judgment when we assume the "bad" choices we see people make are bad *as such*, regardless, especially with people for whom there might not be much to lose. It risks being presumptuous – something thoughtful paternalists would try avoiding – to assume that Bob and others like him fell to where they are because of making stupid decisions and ruining what had once been lives easily capable of going well. That is true in some cases, but again, how do we know which case applies to which person? How would a government know?

Multiple Reasons for Regret

As mentioned previously, defenders of paternalism may cite subsequent regret of (say) many obese people that they should not have eaten so much bad food. While some exhibit regret – especially those with poor impulse control who predictably lament their habits – much still hinges on an individual's preferences across her life. This raises the issue of "opportunity costs". Here are some examples. Should you travel to London or Paris, assuming you can't visit both cities? Should you read this book for another half hour or play Pokémon instead? Should you have lunch today at Boston Market or at Arby's? An opportunity cost of a choice is the value of the most valuable choice out of those that were not taken. By visiting Paris, you miss out on London, so hopefully you expect more out of Paris. The same goes with many other choices facing you. We can't do everything we want to do because resources are scarce. Things might be different if we had all the time, money, and energy in the world . . . but we don't.

With some decisions, like the examples mentioned earlier, opportunity costs are processed at the same time as the benefit we choose to pursue, which can help us to enjoy net benefits without dwelling as much on the sacrificed values. Going to Paris meant I had to miss London. I really wanted to see Big Ben up close, but at least I got to see the Notre Dame Cathedral, and it just wasn't realistic for me to get to see both. The joy of seeing Notre Dame mutes the regret of not seeing Big Ben, so I don't feel all that bad. We will discuss opportunity costs more in Chapter 4.

With other decisions, we experience up-front benefits and downstream costs. All the overeating or smoking you may have enjoyed gave you pleasure for many years before the negative health symptoms began showing up. Another example: sports teams sometimes sign a player in his prime to a long-term contract in order to get him at all, knowing that he will probably be over-the-hill and overpaid for the last part of that expensive contract. Time delays in experiencing the costs of one's decisions can make the costs more vivid and the (past) benefits less so, but they do not necessarily speak to the overall wisdom of the decision. Regret depends on the agent's attitudes and can arise for various reasons tied to what are in the first place her own sometimes changing experiences.

Among other things, regret can be a response to not choosing well in the face of poor habits, or to confrontation of costs one had the chance to consider but failed to make efforts to appreciate after being warned. However, one is mistaken to lament one's unhealthy behavior ("I should have listened!") if, in fact, one enjoyed or otherwise benefitted from the behavior enough to accept the (often foreseeable) costs that have caught up to one. When harms are delayed, regret can be the experience of remaining costs outweighing remaining benefits, but this delay does not speak to the totality of one's costs and benefits across a life.[9]

Health is just one value among many and so trade-offs abound. People's attitudes toward specific costs can vary widely. Regretting what one had preferred to do on balance is trying to have one's cake (so to speak) and eat it too. Now if people want abundant cake *and* no ill effects, and their regret stems from acting on this unrealistic combination of desires, this fact need not show that eating lots of cake is irrational but rather that people are misinformed or self-deceived about the trade-offs involved with their choices. Wanting it both ways is silly, but wanting it both ways doesn't show which way of wanting is the "correct" one. Perhaps we should then aim at letting people become better decision-makers by helping them resolve conflicting preferences, not by forcing their actions away from what we too quickly assume is irrational just because it detracts from all-purpose measures of welfare like health.

Consider Football Fred, who develops diabetes after twenty years of a gluttonous post-retirement diet. Perhaps he could say "I wish I had eaten more salads and cut down on the barbecue" or he could say "It was worth it given all the fun feasts." What he says depends more upon him than what we on the outside can surmise.

Weakness of Will

Defenders of paternalism sometimes highlight an effect known as "hyperbolic discounting". Basically, hyperbolic discounting is when the same agent comes to discount the future at a higher rate once some decision is at hand than she did when that same decision was farther out in the future. Monday morning Dan commits himself to not having dessert on Friday because he is trying to lose weight. He feels pretty confident that he can refuse dessert because he is thinking about the weight he already lost and doesn't want to slow down his win streak.

Then Friday night rolls around and after a nice dinner, the server most evilly wheels out a dessert cart filled with plates of Dan's weaknesses. He suddenly questions his Monday commitment and stops thinking about his long-term weight loss goals. He orders not one but two plates of cake, thus cancelling out all the calories he burned that week. We're observing Dan and think he may have broken his commitment, but should we assume that? These shifts may indeed be evidence of self-control problems, where people who really prefer their long-term good let their short-term cravings get the better of them. Surely there are cases where people suffer weakness of will, where they do what they set out not to do. Our initial sense is that Dan really wanted not to eat the cake, but he let it tempt him against his wiser judgment about keeping his weight down.

Weak will is certainly one hypothesis for his behavior. The challenge, however, is that we observers (and perhaps in some cases Dan himself!) may not know whether he is always weak-willed or sometimes simply changing his mind. People can change their minds without it being a sign of foolishness or poor discipline. Let's say he had a productive week, got a lot done at the office, is feeling good about himself, and the smile on his supervisor's face suggested an upcoming promotion and raise. Maybe Dan is celebrating all his past hard work. Sure, he promised himself last Monday not to splurge, but that was Monday when he didn't know how good his week would turn out.

Suppose instead that his week *sucked*. He spilled coffee on his best suit, his presentation to the board of directors was a disaster, his partner texted that "we need to talk", and his boss yelled at him in front of everyone until he started crying. Maybe now those two slices of cake are a way to bring down his stress and remind himself that there are still nice things in this wild life, despite a bad week. Do you think he made bad choices in either case? It seems he did if we think he's merely weak-willed and broke a promise to himself, but what if he changed his mind instead? How do *we* know?

Let's make things more complicated. Suppose Dan seems to change his mind all the time, telling us (and maybe himself) that he needs to lose weight but then ordering cake. Is that because of a weak will? Is it because he's just one of these guys who is fickle and always changing his mind about things? (Don't you know some people like that?) Maybe there's a third explanation. Perhaps instead it's a sign that Dan does not really prefer what he *claims* to prefer. Like the smoker who claims to want to quit but really might not, Dan feels under pressure to say he should eat healthier because that is the socially acceptable thing to say. He may be signaling or engaging in "cheap talk" about weight loss when he actually prefers to eat cake over losing weight. Preferences revealed by his actions, versus his stated or verbal preferences, add to the information obstacles facing the paternalist, since we may have no way of knowing which preference is Dan's "true" one. Perhaps the saying is true: actions (usually) speak louder than words.

Now perhaps we have other information about Dan, not because we're spies but because we're his friends. We know he hits the gym five times a week, which suggests he is committed to losing weight through exercise but having a harder time with his diet. That could suggest weak will as the best explanation. But . . . might he exercise that much *so that* he can eat more, and he just hasn't mentioned this part to us? People don't just work out to lose weight – they might work out to avoid gaining weight so they can keep eating a lot! With all this up in the air, how would state laws, policies, and regulations know why Dan is acting the way he does, when even his friends aren't sure?

If a drug addict or procrastinator exhibited a pattern of seeking to change but then backsliding, we would have to question the rationality of her waffling and the possibility that she does not control her impulses well. Surely all people face self-control challenges some of the time, and some people face them much of the time, but the key question is whether an informed agent *wants* to keep herself protected from the effects of her hyperbolic discounting. Sometimes the evidence we need is her admission that she wants this protection, but even then, actions may speak louder than words: does she take the simple steps of enrolling in a savings plan or a public commitment to change her behavior? Regardless of what she says, a smoker may through a pattern of behavior reveal an unwillingness to change her ways. We can't know if her unwillingness is a consequence of her addiction or largely a cause of it.

A conflict between stated preferences and revealed preferences can't by itself show that hyperbolic discounters are acting in ways they would rather not act, ways that depart from their own self-defined "true" preferences. That verdict depends on the specific individual, and we may have no clear judgment on whether a person is truly committed or merely paying lip service to changing unhealthy habits. Some people are probably acting irrationally and others are not. How the *bleep* do we know which is which? We at least need more information about particular people and their circumstances.

Procrastination is sometimes a reason many people do not save enough for retirement, but a variety of circumstances can also suggest themselves, which underlines the relevance of informational constraints. People might be paying off debts (student loans, credit card debt, health care expenses). They could be building home equity by paying a mortgage. They could be paying for their children (medical bills, college, etc.). They could be low-income during their prime earning years, living hand-to-mouth (e.g., relatively poor or valuing leisure more). They could have a generous sponsor or be expecting a generous inheritance. Tax incentives could be such as to discourage savings, if say, tax cuts tend to encourage more spending rather than more saving. Some people do not expect to reach or live much longer than typical retirement age. Some don't want to retire and intend to earn an income until death. Some people might prefer to enjoy consumption when they are relatively young.[10] Are you going to enjoy that trip to Europe as much at age 70 as you will at age 30? Some might have extended family to support them once they are unable to earn income. And, of course, some might be genuinely weak-willed, wanting to save more but making bad choices by their own lights because they give in to temptations or procrastinate on savings. They could also be misinformed or ignorant about the possible need to save more, given their values and situation (e.g., bad parenting and education).

Return to our cast of characters that began the chapter. Are any or all of these people making bad choices? If you answered yes to some but no to others, the author would love for you to argue for the distinctions in your responses. If you answered yes to all of them, the author thinks you are being consistent but still demands reasons. If you answered no to all of them . . . you're not off the hook yet. In any case, e-mail the author here and he'll try to get back to you if other deadlines aren't looming: ultrafinite@gmail.com

Our Natural Indeterminacy

Maybe we're not ideally rational, but what if we're deviating from our typical behavior when we appear to make bad choices? Some might object that I am neglecting the role of tendencies in judging a person's rationality. Tendencies are patterns of behavior that people usually exhibit. Maybe you hit the gym three times a week, or maybe you eat Taco Bell three times a week, like clockwork. Philosophers make a distinction between "dispositional" preferences – ones we tend to have – and anomalous preferences, ones that are different from what we tend to have.[11]

This distinction seems proper in many cases. A person we know to value sobriety is probably not making a good choice, given his own beliefs and values, when he binge drinks on a whim. But we also risk overusing the distinction since tendencies are not necessarily fixed across a person's life. People change over time, as defenders of paternalism like Hanna often suggest when advocating for a person's future self against his past decisions. Tendencies can form by the very same patterns of individual choice by which they can also erode.

Dan is about to buy the car he has been planning to buy for months, yet he backs out right before the purchase. Tendencies are indicators of past behavior, but it remains unclear (maybe even to Dan) whether he just has cold feet or instead is in the early stages of changing his preferences and behavior such that he is eroding the intention to buy a car or beginning to replace it with a new, incompatible intention. So his reasons to purchase at the time might be weighty in a backward-looking sense but not weighty in a forward-looking sense, given uncertainty about changes in his outlook or plans in light of new information brought before his attention. (We should take his future tastes into account, right?) Perhaps he glimpsed a lovely but expensive sculpture for sale that morning – one that reminded him of his deceased wife – and began to think more about how having the new car would keep him from being able to afford the sculpture.

These details are best known to Dan – who else could know them, if anyone? Getting cold feet is irrational only if we continue to endorse enough of our other beliefs and values for why we should perform the action about which we now have reluctance. Yet we may not be able to evaluate his choice by assuming these other reasons are fixed. Sticking with a tendency one is beginning to question may just be resistance to change, a status-quo bias that expresses unnecessary conservatism about the options available to one. A person is likely irrational to depart from all his tendencies at once, but it need not follow that his departing from any one tendency is irrational.

Since no sane view denies that agents can rationally change their minds at least sometimes, in light of new information, new circumstances, and/or changing beliefs and values, any view should acknowledge that such shifts must begin at some moment if they are to happen at all. And if they can begin at some moment, why is not the agent himself the judge of whether to persist with or intercept the shift? We may get into trouble if we are too chaotic, since then we may lack any coherent selfhood across time and so can't enjoy any durable experiences or achieved goals as being ourselves at least, but it still doesn't follow that the paternalist is warranted in imposing her view of what particular tendencies the person should be keeping or shifting toward.

Framing effects are evidence of our indefinite nature, and they are one of the most commonly acknowledged biases in the behavioral economics literature. They may often cause and result from our often-indefinite preference orderings.[12] Studies have shown that people react differently to logically equivalent statements, depending on how they are worded. As mentioned before, they will claim to accept potentially quite beneficial surgery if told they have a 9 in 10 chance of living, but some of the same respondents will decline the same surgery if told they have a 1 in 10 chance of dying.[13] What remains unclear is whether a given agent prefers to undergo or decline surgery based on her interpretation of the wording she is given. Most of us are not logic geeks but we all speak a natural language, and logically equivalent statements may still carry distinct meanings given a term known as "conversational implicature".

A statement that anchors on survival may be interpreted to suggest the importance of survival, whereas a statement anchoring on death may be interpreted to suggest the looming possibility of death. Perhaps context should not affect the decision of whether to elect or decline surgery, but in the absence of knowing what a person's "true" preference would be, we (and perhaps she!) have no way of knowing which decision is better for her without having a detailed all-things-considered evaluation of her other (often situation-dependent) judgments.

Matters must be this way if behavioral economists are correct that we are unavoidably influenced by social and sub-conscious factors. What's more, we may not even know what some of our preferences or values are until they are revealed in our decisions and actions.[14] (Think about some decisions you've made before – do you always have in mind beforehand precisely what it is you want to do?) The very situation-dependency of our decisions may tell against coercion rather than for it, sensitive as they are to details beyond our conscious awareness or the observations of an outside party. It depends on the agent whether she or the paternalist should carry out the plan of her actions. Not imposing preferences? Maybe we are. . . .

This leaves us with a puzzle. If there is no neutral way to present information, but we assume people want some level of information, what do we do? Can we not help but influence them to act in some or other foreseeable way even if we don't have any *intention* to steer them in a particular direction? What do we do to help people make the decisions that reflect their own preferences and judgments rather than ours? These are tough questions. Do we draw at random the order in which we frame matters? Do we frame it both ways and hope the one that most reflects their preferences is the one that sticks? Do we resign ourselves to the fact that some people don't have preferences one way or another, and so what they decide may end up being because of random factors such as how we frame things? This may speak to how nudging can better attempt to preserve our freedom to choose in ways coercion does not.

DO EXAMPLES SHOW PATERNALISM IS FALSE?

Defenders of paternalism might agree that a lot of the cases I describe would not support paternalism because, in fact, by intervening we might make a person's life go worse overall. Maybe Bob should be free to smoke, for instance. But perhaps Bob's case is unusual and doesn't describe the typical smoker's life. For typical smokers, perhaps their habit is a net cost and something they shouldn't engage in. Let me sketch some real-life examples that might make paternalism sound more attractive.

Consider rock musicians Jimi Hendrix, Jim Morrison, Janis Joplin, and Kurt Cobain. All of them were tremendously talented and huge influences on rock. All of them also died at age 27. Hendrix and Joplin died of drug overdoses. Cobain committed suicide. The cause of Morrison's death remains unknown, although some have speculated that it was due to heavy alcohol dependence. Did going all-out in life make them larger than life? Is there some kind of romanticism to living fast and dying young? Perhaps. Still, I can't help but think each of their deaths is tragic. If the ghosts of these musicians could speak to us, might at least some if not all of them say they wish they hadn't died that way, and so soon? Might they hope someone had stopped them from the choices that led to these bad outcomes? What do you think?

Finally, let's look at an example from Hanna that poses a rather thorny hard case. This is the case of the Reckless Hiker. You are hanging out at a national park, and you overhear some guy asking a park ranger for maps. You overhear the ranger telling Hiker that they're currently out of maps, but a few of the bridges are dangerous, needing repair, and he should not cross them under any circumstances. But without the map, it's unclear to Hiker which bridges he should not cross, so he'd be wise not to cross any until a map is available. Nevertheless, Hiker decides he'll throw caution to the wind and cross whatever bridge he damn well pleases. Later on, you see him approaching a bridge you know to be dangerous, but which Hiker perceives as only a risk and not a sure danger.

What would you do in this case? Frankly, I would intervene temporarily even if it's an instance of hard paternalism. But why, if I'm a big old anti-paternalist? Because it would be *really weird* if I just let him cross, on the off chance that he would prefer I not stop him. Letting him make this bad choice would be weird in a way that doesn't seem weird in most other cases of opposing paternalism. Now if I had heard him say earlier "Do not stop me" then maybe it would be different.

Hanna is right that we should evaluate the shape of a life, but the future is uncertain. Some want contentment, others excitement. Some want excellence, others just need relief. The answers to all of this? In many cases we don't *know*. It's deeply personal. How can the law decipher? So maybe we should err on the side of letting people be free to make choices, good or bad. I can't help you trying to make my life better when you might make it worse. I *can* help making my life better even when I have the power to muck it up in your absence. I can control making my life better in your absence. I can't control my life going worse in your presence.

One response to this is that since we don't know, maybe we should sometimes err on the side of *caution* with the information we have. That is, we should sometimes stop people from making what are almost certain to be bad choices, like Reckless Hiker. Examples themselves don't give us the answer one way or another. And some of the examples I have provided don't represent those who *are* genuinely struggling with bad choices they would rather not make. Hanna recognizes the limits of examples in settling the question of paternalism:

> I will sometimes appeal to examples to illustrate the claims I am defending. Since these examples are usually intended for illustrative purposes, no one should reject pro-paternalism on the grounds, for instance, that intervention in some of the cases I discuss would do more harm than good, and so forth. Such objections would show only

that the acts and policies in question cannot be justified by the pro-paternalist view, not that pro-paternalism is itself mistaken.[15]

As mentioned before, most contemporary defenders of paternalism agree that the human good mainly comes down to satisfaction of informed preferences. I argued in this chapter that many times it is unclear to us on the outside what a person's preferences actually are, which renders difficult, if not impossible, the judgment of whether they are often making bad choices in light of those preferences. That being said, what about people who really *do* want to stop making certain choices they themselves regard as bad, or would consider bad if they thought about it? I turn to this issue in the next chapter. I can't simply assume every potentially bad choice a person can make is really just a "bad" choice that actually reflects her preferences. That's too easy – there must be some other possibilities.

Three

If one theme of Chapter 2 was that actions may usually be louder than words, surely sometimes words can also be louder than actions. Sometimes people really want to change, to stop their bad habits. But it often takes more work, more effort, to achieve healthier and more prudent goals. It's easy to remain in inertia or be distracted, but getting to where you want in life is not a matter of cruise control. Sarah Conly is right – some of us may even *want to* be forced not to do certain things to relieve ourselves of the responsibility of having to choose to avoid these things.

The philosopher Harry Frankfurt draws a distinction between "first-order" and "second-order" desires.[1] First-order desires are desires about things, experiences, events, states of affairs, and the like. Second-order desires are desires *about desires*. I may have a first-order desire to smoke this entire pack of cigarettes today. At the same time, I may have a second-order *desire not to desire to smoke*. It's not merely the case that I have two conflicting desires. Rather, I don't want to have some of the preferences that I have and act upon. I don't want to be a person who craves nicotine even though I continue to crave it. (Or, if turns out I wish to continue being a smoker, I at least want to have reflected enough on the costs and benefits of smoking that my cravings align with these more reflective second-order desires – in which case I *desire to desire to smoke*.)

So it looks as though there can be many cases in which people's actions and first-order desires do not reflect what they themselves, as flesh-and-blood people, truly desire to do if they thought about it more. Paternalism might be called for by these people's own beliefs and values in such cases. But is this true of everyone? Most people? That's still a difficult question to answer since we can't read their minds. I can't tell what your second-order desires are simply by reading them off your words or actions. Perhaps more importantly, however, even though you may sincerely admit that you should stop making certain choices, that doesn't mean you think it's OK for someone else to *force* you to stop making them. It *may be OK for you to have the freedom to make bad choices if it's not OK for others to stop you.*

Sometimes people act in ways that deviate from how they think they should really act. It would be incredible if all the actions everyone did *always* reflected what they really wanted to do in their heart of hearts, all things considered. Jake has an important medical exam tomorrow morning for which he admits he should try getting a good night's sleep. Instead, he gets hammered and stays up so late that he sleeps in and misses the test. Do we say that Jake really must have wanted to get drunk and put himself at risk of missing the exam after all the work he has already put into his expensive medical school pursuit? Maybe there's no fact of the matter that Jake's choice was objectively bad, but it sure seems bad according to Jake's own self-defined beliefs and values, especially as much as we can gather from his past studious pattern of actions and repeated impassioned claims that his dream is to be a physician. He would likely acknowledge that he made a bad choice – *by his own lights* – to party rather than turn in early. Jake doesn't need us to tell him this the next day when he is staring that F in the face. He sure seems to have let himself down.

Unlike many of the characters discussed in Chapter 2, I can't think of a good way to suggest that Jake really didn't make a bad choice. The writing is on the wall that he did. So if he made a bad choice with really bad consequences – if he got in his own way and thereby undermined one of his most important goals – could there at least be a case in principle for paternalism, even if it's not feasible here? Recall Conly's claim that paternalism is meant to help us from getting in our own way *as we would admit it on reflection*. We can easily imagine a more reflective Jake saying "It was stupid of me to party on such an important night, and now that I've failed out of med school, I really wish someone would have stopped me."

Consider "Neutral Hard Paternalism" (NHP): **whatever you believe and value (that isn't obviously false or crazy), if your chosen actions deviate from that, then it may be proper for someone to interfere with your actions to bring them back into alignment with what you believe and value.** Even if someone doesn't want NHP-based interference in the moment, it doesn't follow that they are opposed to it if they thought things through. NHP is consistent with the subjectivism about welfare that was discussed in Chapter 2. Recall that most contemporary defenders of paternalism don't appeal to some objective good(s) and take that to be the standard for determining when we interfere with someone whose actions deviate from obtaining those goods. Rather, they ascertain as best they can what a person's strongest and most stable preferences are, then use those as the standard for determining whether we interfere, should a person's actions depart from those preferences.

Thus, NHP seems appealing because it doesn't seem to impose values. The paternalist is merely forcing you not to do what you admit you shouldn't do. Again, there are often situations where there is no feasible way to interfere without being intrusive (hence the "may be" in the formulation of NHP). But the main point is that NHP might be true in principle even if it's not always applicable. It wasn't OK by Jake's own lights for him to choose getting drunk, and so it might be permissible to stop Jake if circumstances made sense. So, does it follow that all of us should accept NHP? When we admit some of our choices are bad, are we thereby open to endorsing this principle? Is there no alternative some of us might embrace?

Consider the following anti-NHP principle: **Whatever I believe and value (that isn't obviously false or crazy), if my chosen actions deviate from that, then it is *my responsibility* to stop acting that way and bring my actions back into alignment with what I believe and value**. This principle reflects what I will call "Capacity for Decision-making" (CAD). If you don't take anything else away from this discussion, consider this line to capture the essence of CAD: "I find value in having the freedom to make bad choices because having that freedom renders my good free choices *even more valuable* – they originate from my own initiative and not someone else's coercion."

That is, if a paternalist attempts to coerce me on the grounds that I should be committed to accepting NHP as a guiding principle, I can rebut her by appealing to this view about what makes my life most valuable. I can say to the paternalist: "I know what I've been doing goes against my own beliefs and values. But I should be the one to knock it off rather than be coerced by you. That enhances the value of my good choices."

Before describing CAD in greater detail, I will offer two analogies. The first involves an aspiring novelist who is committed to writing the best work he can compose, and who seeks to have the final say on everything in his book. In other words, the novelist seeks ultimate artistic control over the choices and decisions about the content of his manuscript. He is quite open to advice about changes, but ultimately he decides whether to take that advice. We should not be surprised if the novelist took offense at an editor's uninvited changes to and subsequent publication of his story. Even if the changes vastly improved the story and afforded our novelist fame, fortune, and increased opportunities to write, we would still think him reasonable to demand that any of his published works be a product of his own fallible artistic judgment, and that any suggested changes require his permission. Much of the value of their activity to artists is that the product comes from their control over their artistic decisions. Leaving aside those who actually want ghost writers, it would be unusual for an artist not in collaboration with others to give priority to anyone else completing the artwork, regardless of how much or little alteration is done by others.[2]

Now, CAD applies this "independence" feature of artistic activity to all aspects of a person's life which turn on his free choices about actions largely affecting himself. It seems plausible that some people (not everyone, but some!) might value the sort of independence and responsibility for their lives *as such*, even for seemingly mundane choices, that an independent artist seeks for his aesthetic undertakings. These people value pursuit of their goals partly as a function of their making free choices and decisions, for better or worse and however seemingly mundane, in all areas of their lives at each waking moment. They are open to advice and persuasion about how to make better choices, but they find it important to have the final say over all their largely self-regarding choices. Given his commitment, what good reasons would a proponent of CAD (henceforth, a "CADet") have not to demand noninterference with any of his voluntary actions, provided those actions violate no rights of others?

A possible answer to this question comes from noting that the novelist analogy is not perfect. While it shows a person can prefer independence over someone else's partial contributions, it doesn't quite match the consequences of failure to refrain from severely harmful actions nor the loss of freedom a CADet faces within paternalistic constraints. An independent writer who ignores sage advice and thus fails to craft the best novel he can possibly write is stuck with a substandard product, whereas the failed CADet can risk significant harms to his well-being if he turns out to make bad choices. More is typically at stake for a failed CADet than a failed novelist. Further, the editor would only have (say) altered the content of the novelist's work had he written substandard material. Since the pinnacle of success is when a writer independently crafts a work needing no alteration, he (allegedly) loses nothing under the editor's power. While it is not perfect, however, the analogy emphasizes the value some persons can find through free, independent, and rational activity under their control.

The second analogy fills in the point begun earlier. It involves a remotely controlled brain manipulation device that paternalists can use (or threaten to use) every time the target seems about to make a bad choice. The device has two settings. Let's first imagine a more powerful setting that blocks Fred's ability to choose poorly, forces him to act in the right manner, and leaves him alone whenever he is already making the proper choices. Even in situations where Fred chooses the proper course, it is not a fully free choice compared to the amount of freedom from coercion that non-use of the paternalist's device could grant him – using the device will not let him act on other than the correct choice.

Granted, Fred still has some measure of freedom in the sense that he is able to initiate his actions or not, rather than defaulting and thus allowing the device to initiate the actions. But Fred wants more options than merely: (1) choose to do action A, or (2) choose not to do A and thus trigger the device. Instead, he wants options: (1) choose to do A, (2) choose not to do A (without triggering any device), or (3) choose to do not-A. I doubt even those liberals who are fine with paternalism would hold that paternalists can permissibly use this device on us. Usage of the device, however infrequent, is too intrusive because it never allows people the freedom to act properly *both* by their own initiative *and* when they could do otherwise. Such people may not have adequate control over their lives with the device ready to override their decisions.

Baseball fans: What if we controlled a batter that way? Wouldn't the game lose a lot of its meaning? Aaron Judge hits a home run to win the game, and in the postgame interview he says: "I'd like to thank my remote controller for making me swing at a pitch I may have taken for a strike. Although I didn't accomplish the homer, the ball still left the park, so what difference does it make whether it was me or my baseball overlord?" How meaningful would this be? How absurd? Sports as we know it always measures athletic performance in the face of possible failure. Otherwise, why not just let robots play . . . and how boring would that become? (OK, actual robot baseball might be pretty great too, but human baseball has attracted millions of fans for over a century. You can decide which game you would pay more to see over time.)

Suppose a less powerful setting does not directly force someone to do the right thing but only incapacitates her *until* she chooses to act properly. A paternalist declares the device will incapacitate Haley every time she is about to choose or act unwisely by her own standards. This way, she is not always forced to act rightly since (at least sometimes) she can choose to remain incapacitated. This again seems too intrusive, however, because the threat of incapacity is itself strongly coercive. For instance, it would imply a paternalistic editor could freeze Haley whenever she was about to write a less than adequate bit of prose and keep her frozen until she wrote adequately. Why should Haley find this situation unacceptable? Part of the value she takes in artistic achievement – what makes it *her* achievement – is not merely human creativity as such, but also that she had the freedom to choose otherwise in *her* creative endeavor, to make bad artistic choices, to be lazy, and so forth.

Following are four features of CAD:

1   CAD counts as free those actions over which a person has at least minimum control. More specifically, this person has (or takes himself to have) control over his thought processes and actions, which always includes the ability *not* to think or act. On this view, even unreflective choices and actions can qualify as free and voluntary since the person controls whether or not to act reflectively. (The Canadian rock band Rush has a line in their song "Freewill" that speaks to this: "If you choose not to decide, you still have made a choice.") In accepting this account of freedom, the CADet has a reasonable though controversial view. Not everyone is a CADet, obviously, and that's fine! Some people want paternalistic protection. But some people might not want it.

2   CAD also holds that all the CADet's largely self-regarding actions be freely chosen *and* consistent with whatever his goals may be. So he should actually make good choices that serve his goals, even though he should be free to make even very bad choices. With this freedom, he clearly should not make truly bad choices that set back his goals and overall interests. On this point, CADets and paternalists can agree that bad choices are, well, bad. But the CADet prizes personal responsibility for those choices in all avenues of his life: staying focused on the task at hand, applying himself rather than succumbing to laziness, staying alert to harms and detractions from his well-being, asking for help when he deems it preferable, etc. What is of the highest value to the CADet is not merely that his actions are his own, but also that his actions are *his-own-and-good*. It is important not to separate these two elements. If *all* he cared about was that his actions were his own, then he could embrace all kinds of unintelligible behavior, while rational goal pursuit would make no difference to him. He could just choose to count grass blades, or walk in circles all day, or stab himself with forks. ("Hey! I'm not fork-stabbing *you*, so what business is it of yours?") This is not an accurate picture of what CAD defends. But neither is he only concerned that his actions be correct, period (and so forcibly corrected when improper.) His greatest good, his ideal, is that his goals are always freely-aimed-at-by-his-own-rational-efforts. Again, he would rather be free to fail than be coerced *not* to fail by paternalistic force.

3   Unless the CADet is free to choose rationally in the face of irrational alternatives made possible by noninterference, he can't know whether *he* would have attained his ideal by his own efforts or whether he is partly motivated, say, by

an expectation of paternalistic constraint. A CADet prevented from having the freedom to make certain choices is guaranteed (against his will) not to have certain possibilities of failure that he would have if granted freedom from interference. Under paternalism, he is aware that his life is at least partly someone else's (the paternalist's) project.[3] His opposition to the threat of paternalism remains even if the CADet *never* acts irrationally beneath that threat, since he can never know that he did the right thing by his own initiative or because the threats of paternalistic force motivated him to make good choices. Hence, the CADet rejects being subjected to paternalistic laws and policies *even* if he were always to make good choices under their threat of enforcement.

4   Putting one's life together coherently is a challenge from the long-range perspective, though any *particular* action comprising one's life may not be challenging in itself. By analogy, making a single free throw shot in basketball is not at all difficult. Making one hundred shots in a row, however, is difficult, something even most professional players can rarely do.[4] Likewise, it is no special accomplishment to perform an easy task, but persons typically retain the freedom not to perform it. To go through one's life always making good decisions (at least with the information at one's disposal) when one could have done otherwise adds up to a challenging goal CADets may aim to accomplish. This is an instance of what philosophers call an "emergent property" – a property contained by the whole that may not belong to any of its constituent parts. Seen in this light, the freedom to choose whether or not to wear a seat belt – *even when* one's values commit one to buckling up – need not look trivial. When I choose to put

on the seat belt that saves me from crashing through the windshield that would have killed me and thus prevented thirty more years of good living . . . I am not at all making a trivial choice. Extend this consideration to all the other good choices I can make in light of possible bad choices. It is not clear how a "relatively trivial" freedom to choose at any one moment amounts to triviality when considering how those choices add up over a long stretch of time.

CADETS VERSUS PATERNALISTS

People can have other reasons, such as commitment to a norm, that do not easily translate into goal-based reasons for following a certain view. For instance, a CADet might see CAD as most consistent with how she thinks of herself as a person. She feels resentment at the (threat of) paternalistic interference not so much because it obstructs her project of acting freely at all times – although it might – but because the (threat of) interference undermines her ability to act on her sincere view of what it means to be a free and equal moral person.

Our beliefs and judgments may sometimes have little to do with pursuing goals, but we would object to those beliefs or judgments being overridden without what we would recognize as a decisive reason. If paternalism merely obstructed an agent's pursuit of goals, then resentment at paternalism would be an inappropriate attitude, as misplaced as my feeling resentment at my far abler opponent for obstructing my goal of winning our tennis match. Yet we are left with the sense that resentment is at least sometimes a proper response to such coercion. (I will say more about this in the next chapter, when I discuss the risk of coercion – including paternalism – that presumes commitments a person need not have.)

To borrow Stanley Benn's example: Al acknowledges that his splitting pebbles all day is worthless, yet he rightly feels resentment when Beth keeps interfering with his activity even on the grounds that *Al himself* knows better than to engage in that worthless activity.[5] Al properly feels resentment if Beth doesn't give *him* good reasons for her intervening – reasons that follow from *his own* beliefs and judgments, not only hers. She might tell him that she thinks he is wasting his time, but unless he has good reason to admit that he shouldn't be *free* to waste his time, why should her dissenting view alone give her permission to stop him?

This suggests someone opposed to NHP has other reasons, besides merely appeals to *goals*, for opposing what he sees as the paternalist's imposition of a view that he rejects. And Al rejects the following rationale: "If you (Al) are doing something that sets back your interests in a way that even you would acknowledge, it might be OK for me (Beth) to intervene." Al can admit he should stop wasting time with pebble-splitting, but he also believes that *he*, not Beth, should be the one to stop the activity so he can get on to something more worthwhile. Independent of goal-based considerations, Beth's intervention is an instance where she substitutes her own, paternalistic, judgment for Al's view that he should *still be free* to waste his time at a meaningless activity – even though he also admits he shouldn't be wasting his time! Your *judgment* about what you should be free to do is a separate issue from your pursuit of goals.

CAD cuts across many views. Paternalism, even NHP, is unjustified to the CADet not merely because it is paternalistic as such, but because it is based on the view that a person's conception of himself as having the ability to make good choices at each moment – and his referring to this ability in making a moral claim on another not to interfere even when he could make bad choices – *does not count* as a legitimate veto of a coercive law. Part of his view of the good life for himself is that he makes his choices in an environment where others are not limiting those choices for his own benefit. But the paternalist decides, on behalf of the target, what elements of his agency *do* count as relevant to permissible interference with his freely chosen actions.

The paternalist thinks some potentially harmful freedoms of choice are trivial and so should be stopped – the CADet disagrees. Shouldn't the tiebreaker go to the CADet with regard to his own life? I am engaging NHP on its own premise that the wrongfulness of using a controversial view of the good (even one the coercer personally thinks is true or correct) to override another's action motivates the search for a neutral subjectivist principle. Yet if NHP aims to respect someone's conception of the good as *that person* defines it, it seems odd not to extend respect to that person's conception of his personhood, which is just as much a reflection (if not more) of his judgment as are his preferences about what values to pursue or what flavor of ice cream to eat.

Now suppose some people also endorse CAD because this life may well be a valuable challenge. It requires CADets *not* to rely on others' coercive interventions when they themselves are able to make good choices. At every moment the CADet might adopt the "maximax" approach of aiming for the highest payoff of a freely chosen and successfully performed action when he could have chosen much worse – even if, after the fact, the agent makes a bad choice by his own lights. This agent prefers to have the freedom to fail as a *precondition* of having the ability to succeed without reliance on paternalism as a failsafe. Choosing well in the face of being able to have chosen badly is, for some, a hallmark condition of moral agency *and* the good life.

For CADets, even a successful life led beneath the paternalist's cloud is less preferred than a successful life free of such a cloud. They prefer having the freedom to act on their own choices over coercive laws and regulations that keep them from making such choices. They prefer having the *freedom* to fail even though of course they do not prefer to *actually* fail.

To support this latter point, consider the following ranking of life outcomes a CADet can have, listed from best to worst:

100.1 (or more) units of utility – where we understand "utility" in a very wide sense to include a sum of elements like well-being, pleasure and happiness, absence of stress, preference satisfaction, and living by one's judgments – for freely making the right choices at each moment, free of paternalistic coercion or its threat, and for acting on one's personal conception of how best to live

100 units of utility for always making good choices at each moment, but under a paternalistic threat

90 units of utility for generally making good choices but occasionally being subject to paternalism to prevent the possibility of making certain bad choices

0 units of utility for making severe and irreversible self-harmful choices that lead to personal tragedy

From this ranking one might think we summon NHP in just those instances where freedom to make a bad choice would put one at risk of realizing no more than 90 units. However, a "maximaxer" (our CADet) or "maximiner" (people who are fine with some degree of paternalism) can bundle their preference rankings into different pairs of each view's highest to lowest payoffs as follows:

CAD (100.1 or more, 0)
NHP-consistent view (100, 90)

The maximiner chooses the policy that awards the highest payoff among all possible worst outcomes, so she prefers NHP views (90) over CAD (0). She would rather not be left free to make terrible choices. But the maximaxer chooses the policy that awards the highest payoff among all possible best outcomes, so he prefers CAD (100.1 or more) to NHP views (100).

Of course, not just any maximax behavior is reasonable. One might object that it is foolish to prefer CAD over NHP if CAD's best outcome is only a tiny bit better the best outcome under NHP, especially given the risk of not being protected from making terrible choices. Imagine a billionaire who was willing to risk losing all of his wealth on the chance to win only 100 more dollars at a Roulette table. We would rightly question this person's sanity, so shouldn't we regard the CADet in the same light? No. The main reason is that the CADet is in control of his "risk" of whether he chooses the kinds of self-harmful acts paternalism is meant to prevent. One can't control the outcome of a Roulette wheel's spin – that's pure luck, by contrast. (Nonetheless, the rich gambler should still be free to make a tremendously dumb choice that will likely turn out horribly for him.)

Now saying the "risk" is controlled by the CADet's free choice assumes that he acts with sufficient control over his choice, which raises the important issue of how we can determine whether an act meets such a condition. I will put this issue on hold until Chapter 5 since appeal to CAD . . . well, it depends. Soft paternalism is still an issue we should explore. CAD merely claims that if a person is sufficiently in control of his choices (that is, not sufficiently impaired so as not to make the choices truly his own), then we can regard the risks he assumes as also his responsibility.

HARMS AND TIME LAGS

At this point, a paternalist might press the issue of "time lag" harms and how these might bear on self-harmed people's attitudes after the fact. For certain harms, there is a delay between when a very bad choice is made and when the terrible harm occurs. For an extreme example, consider people who have chosen to leap to their deaths. One percent of people known to have jumped off the Golden Gate Bridge have lived to tell about it. One's body hits the water at over seventy miles an hour – the force of impact is lethal almost every time. Kevin Hines is a real-life person who survived a suicide attempt off that bridge. He said that as soon as he jumped, he knew he had just made a terrible decision, and he claims that other survivors of the jump have told him the same. So in cases like these, if we have good evidence (their own words) that people immediately regret what they just did, paternalists can use this regret to argue that people don't really want to make certain horrible choices, and so it is OK to stop them beforehand if we have time to save them. Hines had no safety net to catch his fall and no bystander to prevent him from jumping. But maybe there are cases where laws and regulations can prevent people from doing something bad, especially if they themselves acknowledge as much.

Besides, even if a CADet made a tragically bad choice, they would no longer even have access to the benefits CAD promises (namely, when CADets freely make good choices and freely avoid bad ones). Their worst choices can make things a done deal, which might then show that most people are not actually committed to radical anti-paternalism in the first place. The jumper who decides on the fall down that this was a bad idea and wants a safety net, or the alcoholic with cirrhosis who wishes he had been forced to stop drinking years earlier, illustrate that we cannot easily separate the subsequent regret and retroactive authorization of their future selves from the past commitment (if any) to CAD's radical freedom of choice. If so, most people might actually be committed to endorsing paternalistic interference *beforehand*.

Once you have made a bad choice and aren't committed to seeing it through – and why would you be so committed? – you would be open to opportunities to undo that choice. But if you are open to undoing the bad choice, why wouldn't you also be open to not being allowed to choose badly in the first place? Desiring freedom of choice means that you are also committed to facing up to the consequences of those choices. But if you change your mind after making a bad choice, then maybe you aren't really committed to the freedom of making that bad choice in the first place. "Give me the freedom to jump without a net, but once I jump put that net out there" seems, if not incoherent, then bizarre. Why not just have the net ready beforehand? So is it a non-starter to be a CADet, at least for some severe harms like these time lag ones?

This does not follow, however. That one would change one's mind and seek help *after* making a bad choice does not show that one doesn't value having the *freedom* to make bad choices – just that one also acknowledges one ought to not make bad choices. Several considerations support this point. First, there is the matter of case-by-case details. Time lag harms may pose a challenge to my anti-paternalistic argument, but if so, this is because of both their delayed nature and also the near-guarantee of severe harm if the bad choice is made, along with the availability of a rescuer during the lag. In these cases, interventions *after* she makes a bad choice might be justified to the agent if her commitments are so aligned. But this at least does not support more standard cases of paternalism, such as anti-smoking laws where severe and immediate harms are not guaranteed to smokers.

Second, we should not assume that the person even afterward must be committed to others helping her undo the bad choice – if she is willing to take responsibility, and her reasons for CAD run through this responsibility, then even if she would prefer not to have made the bad choice, she may remain committed to seeing it through: "I did it – now I need to live (or die) with the bad choice I made." (But *would* anyone say this?)

The third consideration is most key, however. A person can say consistently: "I regret making the choice, but I don't regret having had the freedom to make it. That's consistent with me wanting to be saved afterward when I'm helpless!" The assignment of property rights can clear up some ambiguities since there isn't a blanket right against paternalism across all situations. Joe may not have the right to jump from a building he doesn't own onto a ground he also does not own. Rescuers concerned with Joe might permissibly prevent him from jumping or catch him if he does. By contrast, he might have that right on his own property and rescuers may not trespass to save him. I may have the right to overindulge on Twinkies in my house, and my concerned friend can't stop me on my property. But maybe my friend can stop me from eating all the Twinkies in her house. If I don't like it, I can leave.

So far in the book I have talked about why even paternalists will say it's OK to make mildly bad choices, especially when we and others can learn from them (Chapter 1), why it's OK to make choices that aren't necessarily bad after all (Chapter 2), and in this chapter why it's OK to make even very bad choices because it's not OK for others to interfere with CADets. But what gives? Most of us are probably not full-blooded CADets across all domains of our lives. What about those of us who may not be committed to CAD with regard to certain potentially bad choices? I will tackle this question in the next chapter.

Four

Is it OK to be free to make bad choices even if you aren't already a CADet? In this chapter I argue yes — because it's not OK for defenders of paternalism to assume people are thereby *already* committed to endorsing paternalism in the mere absence of a CAD commitment. Pro-paternalism isn't the default view and shouldn't be assumed as such. The same goes for assuming many other views are default ones. The main reason is that the ways we form our views are subject to all kinds of complexities and costs, as I will discuss later. We don't come to most of our views effortlessly or in a vacuum.

Now the reason for what may seem like a detour in this chapter is that I don't want to rig the argument against paternalism. Paternalism versus CAD is just one disagreement among many that people can have, so I wish first to show more generally how these disagreements may come about where nobody is clearly mistaken.

A defender of paternalism might respond that not many people are likely committed to acting on the CAD view, at least not in all circumstances. If they're in the minority, perhaps they can be legitimately subject to "democratic paternalism" if voters decide that the cost to CADets of infringements on their freedom is well worth the anticipated benefits of preventing everyone from certain self-harmful behaviors. Or, perhaps instead CADets (and only they) can be *exempted* from paternalistic laws to which the rest of us are bound. These responses sound powerful because they limit themselves to evaluating paternalism on the grounds of what values it can overall promote (or harms it can overall prevent). On a bene-fit/cost analysis, the right thing to do is to generate the most overall good.

This is not the only way to think about right and wrong actions, though. Recall concerns in Chapter 3 about *judgement substitution*, independent of frustrating a person's preference satisfaction or their prior commitment to an ideal like CAD. Coercion needn't be worrisome *as such* (although it might be). Rather, it is problematic when employed to override the judg-ments people may form, the basis of their having good reason to prefer, value, or believe something if given the chance. Even if we exempt the supposed minority of CADets from paternal-istic schemes, there is still likely to be a significant number of other people who, while they don't *already* accept CAD, are also not committed to rejecting it, and so thereby are *not* already committed to accepting a paternalistic rationale either. Call them the "Middle People". Is it OK for Middle People to be free to make bad choices? Is it not OK to coerce Middle People not to make certain bad choices? My claim is that "yes" is the answer to both questions.

First, some background thoughts. Here are a few examples of other things many people aren't committed to accept-ing but aren't thereby committed to rejecting: whether Tom Brady is the best quarterback ever, whether that new local arena should be built with taxpayer money, whether there are 180,003 spiders in Peoria, whether one should convert to Judaism, whether one should write one's aunt on the hol-idays, etc.

Would it be OK to try substituting judgment in these cases? If not, why would it be OK when paternalism is involved? For these Middle People, paternalists are substituting their own judgments that the default view for everyone should be pro-paternalist unless shown otherwise (say, through a prior commitment to CAD). But since we are moral equals, by what authority can those who don't know the Middle People infringe on them with a rationale the latter do not (and need not) hold? It would seem that I get to decide my reasons and values, you get to decide yours, etc. as long as our reasons and values allow us to get along peacefully and with mutual benefit and respect. If you want paternalism for yourself, but I don't already want it for myself, why should I be subject to the paternalism you seek?

Let's distinguish between two standards for when coercion might more generally be justified to someone who is coerced by a law or policy, paternalistic or otherwise. The first and more demanding standard for justifying coercion I'll call "Acceptability": **A law or regulation may rightly limit a person's liberty only if that person's beliefs and values give her decisive reason to *accept* the rationale for that law or regulation**.

The second and less demanding standard I'll call "Rejectability": **A law or regulation may rightly limit a person's liberty only if that person's beliefs and values do not give her decisive reason to *reject* the rationale for that law or regulation**.

For example, I may lack decisive reason to reject the view that Tom Brady is the greatest quarterback ever, but that doesn't mean that I thus have decisive reason to accept the view that Brady is the best quarterback ever. But why does this distinction matter with regard to making bad choices? As we will see,

Acceptability restricts the scope of what counts as justified coercion more than Rejectability, so it will be harder to justify paternalism under Acceptability standards.

Lacking decisive reason to reject a view at a given time does not mean one thereby has decisive reason to accept it either. Maybe you've thought about the view but haven't made up your mind (you're torn between whether Tom Brady or Joe Montana is the best quarterback ever). Maybe you're aware of the view but have never taken the time to think about it (you know of the debate but you don't really care about football). Maybe you're not even aware of the view because you've never had an occasion to be aware of it (you've never heard of football or this Brady guy, and you don't know what a quarterback is).

Now replace the quarterback issue with the debate between paternalists and CADets. Maybe you've thought about the views but haven't made up your mind (you're torn between whether openness to paternalism or instead openness to CAD is the better approach). Maybe you're aware of paternalism and CAD but have never taken the time to think about them (you know of the debate but haven't gotten around to considering how it applies to you). Maybe you're not even aware of the debate because you've never had an occasion to be aware of it (you've never heard of paternalism or CAD).

Here's the thing: if we use a Rejectability standard, it's possible that you're minding your own business, having never thought about CAD, and then bam! . . . your liberty to make certain bad choices is limited by a paternalistic law *just because* you thus currently lack decisive reason to reject paternalism. However, you also don't have a decisive reason to *accept* the law or regulation because you're undecided on the debate or even unaware of it. Defenders of an Acceptability standard would retort that this seems too easy a route to claiming it's OK to stop people from making bad choices – they've never really considered the debate, so how is that fair?

Paternalists concerned about imposing external preferences should be at least as concerned with judgement substitution, assuming the pro-paternalist view is held as the default. They should not be satisfied with Rejectability. It's not OK for someone else to prevent your freedom to make a bad choice on the mere assumption that you accept paternalistic views as the default unless shown otherwise. In this sense, it's legally OK – maybe not morally or rationally OK – to make bad choices when it's not OK for someone else to stop you. Likewise, it's legally OK to break a promise to your friend that you'll pick him up from the airport, but it's not morally OK to disappoint his legitimate expectations because you suddenly didn't feel like doing what you promised.

Now there may be a final class of people who are committed to accepting the paternalistic view under many circumstances. In this case, paternalistic coercion on such a view may be permissible because it already aligns with their judgment. They reject CAD and perhaps thereby are committed to accepting paternalism. Indeed, if there were no known defeaters of paternalistic rationales such as CAD, then those rationales might be in play as justifiable to everyone on Acceptability grounds. Everyone would be committed to accepting paternalism as the default because there are no other reasonable options to rebut it!

Now I'd like to dig into why I find so important this distinction between Rejectability and Acceptability, between lacking decisive reason to reject and having decisive reason to accept certain views. Otherwise, it's unclear why Acceptability is clearly preferable.

THE BURDENS OF FORMING JUDGMENTS

In a liberal democracy, each of us has a major say over the reasons we have for believing and acting as we do. This leads us to disagree a lot about the best kind of life, since our various beliefs, values, and experiences lead us to divergent conceptions of what is best.[1] We might *want* others to see the world and live their lives the same way as us, but we risk imposing our views on them if we insist they do. Access to the reasons we have is crucial for us to have some reliable way of distinguishing between our own say and another's imposition of what *they* think we should believe or how we should act. Someone else simply appealing to some reason or other may provide us no access for why *we* should have this as a good reason, given our beliefs, values, and ways of thinking and experiencing. An atheist may lack good reason to accept Jesus Christ as his lord and savior. A Christian may lack good reason to accept atheism. But why is this the case if someone (maybe both) has to be wrong here about the divinity (or lack) of Christ?

The philosopher John Rawls identifies what he called the "burdens of judgment".[2] We are limited in our ability to collect information and form beliefs from that information. And there is lots of info out there to process. There are different ways of thinking and coming to conclusions, different experiences, and different perspectives. Many of these diverse ways are not clearly wrong, even if they are at odds with each other. The way we come to these beliefs may depend on where we are situated, which differs from person to person – there may not be some universal and objective experience from which we all draw the same inferences. Some people might believe that beauty is the most important value to pursue, but others might think knowledge, or athletic prowess, or moral virtue, or pleasure, or friendships are of utmost importance. Who's right? Perhaps there is a truth of the matter, like there is for scientific facts, but how do we know *who* has the truth about the good life? Lots of very smart people for thousands of years sincerely insisted that they had the truth on some value judgment or other– and many very smart people today still disagree with each other about these!

What's more, there may not be a *single* truth. "Pluralism" about values is the view that there can be multiple fundamental sources of good. We might all agree that beauty, knowledge, freedom, wisdom, athleticism, and so forth are important and worth pursuing, but we differ in how we rank these values against each other. Albert Einstein may have valued knowledge more than athleticism, whereas LeBron James may value athleticism more than knowledge. A CADet may value his freedom of choice more highly than someone who is open to receiving paternalistic coercion. But even if there is some universal True, Correct, or Best value out there, how we come to value things in different ways is probably a function of the different worlds we inherit. Different strokes for different folks – and remember that most defenders of paternalism agree that values are subjective not objective.

The philosopher Gilbert Harman describes how we come to believe what we believe:

> [y]ou start from where you are, with your present beliefs and intentions. Rationality or reasonableness then consists in trying to make improvements in your view. Your initial beliefs and intentions have a privileged position in the sense that you begin with them rather than with nothing at all or with a special privileged part of those beliefs and intentions serving as data.[3]

But don't we make lots of mistakes? Certainly.

We can filter out an actual person's obviously false beliefs, clearly logical errors, and so on. But correcting for obvious faults still leaves intact much of that person's beliefs and values – and the different questions people choose to pursue at different times – so it's unclear what direction we can or should go for inferring his further beliefs and values. We risk imposing foreign reasons or views on people if we assume what they would likely believe, given such factors as limited information and what factors I will argue most shape our way of forming judgments: search, time, energy, and opportunity costs. These factors will also affect whether people will come to have warmer or colder attitudes toward something like paternalism and limiting bad choices.

In trying to find out what to believe, many times our search must be limited to where the light of evidence is already shining, even if better reasons are lurking (or hidden deep) in the shadows of what we don't yet see. Search costs involve figuring out what you are looking for and trying to find it, sometimes in the light but sometimes in the darkness too. This would not be an issue if knowledge were merely information already at our disposal. If we could simply Google what would be the best life to live, or whether there's a God, or what (if any) religion is the *best* one to practice – then things would be much easier. Maybe there's a fact of the matter out there that applies to everyone, but how can any of us be so confident that we know what it is, especially when so many smart have people disagreed for hundreds and thousands of years about whether God exists, or which god(s) exist, or what is the best way to live?

Searches for truth involve the additional cost of *time*, and even more challenging, we do not typically know how long a successful search will take. It would be easier if all searches came with a built-in time of arrival – "you will figure out what you're seeking in six days if you keep at it" – but we know this isn't the case. So we can't rationally plan our searches according to a reliable timeline *even* if we always find the truth eventually, which of course we don't.

In addition, all of this searching takes energy. We are not efficient calculating machines that get fed an endless source of power. We literally require glucose for the effort needed to think clearly and act effectively, and this is a limited resource.[4] These costs highlight why caution is not just a good attitude to have toward one's beliefs, but also toward others' beliefs. Ironically, acknowledging other people's cognitive limitations can increase our appreciation and respect for them lacking access to some True and Correct judgments or rankings of values that we should all adopt. There might be "too much choice", but that fact alone doesn't tell us *what* to choose, believe, or do. Nor does it imply that another may choose on our behalf or impose views on us without regard for whether *we* would come to accept those views without imposition.

We must take seriously the scarcity of resources available to any individual or group trying to figure out what to believe and value, but there is yet one more cost involved. Considering alternative options and acting on such considerations takes not only energy and time, it also keeps one from deliberating or acting in any number of *alternative* ways within one's choice set – opportunity costs. This observation is nothing new, but its significance has drawn increasing support in psychological studies. Recent evidence on "decision fatigue" reveals that we can't costlessly deliberate and decide, that each decision and action saps us of some mental energy.[5] Such depletion, and alternatives not taken, suggest why our cognitive limitations require us to economize on our mental exertions, and these limits inherently affect what we come to believe and value.

What a person regards as worth pondering or pursuing often depends on her situation at each moment, which differs from person to person. This may seem a trite observation, but an important result of this is that an Acceptability standard is almost unavoidably tied to her more closely accessible reasons since keeping them in mind requires fewer of the costs discussed previously. The further out her potential reasons, however, the less weighty they generally are for how she ought to act in her current situation.

This fact reflects the more benign aspect of status-quo and confirmation biases. Even the most skeptical inquirers must hold on to a core set of possibly false views to have anywhere to go on in their future thoughts. Often we should withhold judgment when the evidence either way isn't clear, but sometimes we should revise our beliefs when confronted with contrary evidence. Belief revision implies initial endorsement without decisive evidence. Mere stubbornness need not be why we hold onto what we believe. The further out we go, the more costs we tend to face, and so the more we tend to lack reason to accept or reject some consideration even if there is, out there somewhere, some fact of the matter beyond our current grasp.

Where am I going with all this?

SHIFTING JUDGMENTS

Let's make things more concrete. Imagine Joe lacks decisive reason either to reject or accept the view that he should eat an apple for five minutes each day. The opportunity cost of eating an apple – even deliberating momentarily about whether to do so – is the time and energy he could have used doing his next most-preferred activity. We typically identify what he would have done by identifying his preferences as he states them or reveals them in his actions. But Joe also lacks reason to reject engaging in any of infinitely many other possible actions, some of which he might discover to be more valuable if he tried them.

However, he faces unavoidable opportunity costs not only in performing the actions themselves but also in searching for, thinking about, and deciding which other actions he might perform. We cannot simply read off his current actual preferences and see whether he is committed to accepting or rejecting apple consumption since information about these alternatives might lie beyond even Joe's awareness. Sufficiently informed commitment to an action is one's acceptance that the opportunity costs of performing that action are worth bearing, either as a matter of deliberation or as a matter of performing the action itself.[6]

To illustrate, suppose your initial reason R1 is a sort of early opposition to coercive paternalism ("Don't tread on me!") for which you can't yet tell a compelling story. It's just sort of a gut-level disgust at what you think are nanny state busybodies who should mind their own business. But when pressed to elaborate on why you feel this way, you aren't able to say much more. Without that articulation, you are perhaps open to R2, some paternalistic view, along with a new appreciation of risks and harms. You don't come all the way around to accepting some paternalistic view, but perhaps you read Hanna or Conly's book, and at least your confidence in the view that you should be free to make certain bad choices becomes understandably shaken.

However, let's say you were then to pick up this book and become unsatisfied with R2 (the author can dream, right?). You then become committed to R3, say, a philosophical commitment to CAD. So, over this stretch of time, you start out with a gut-level opposition to paternalism (R1), shift to a more informed non-rejection (but not acceptance) of paternalism (R2), and then shift to a more informed opposition to paternalism (R3) owing to now having decisive reason to accept CAD, given your revised beliefs and judgments. And maybe someday you'll find R4 and change your mind again . . . it's a never-ending process!

At each stage, it seems you ought not to accept paternalism. Perhaps it's simply by chance that you picked up this book and were convinced – otherwise, you might have remained at R2 and lacked reason to reject or accept paternalistic laws. But here's the problem: if you stayed at R2, then Rejectability holds that you might be permissibly subject to paternalistic laws and regulations simply because you *lacked* decisive reason to reject those rationales at the time. Rejectability risks closing off options open to your judgment by imposing on you another's beliefs, values, or preference rankings that may bear no relation to what your deliberation and action would have been without that intervention. To that degree you're subject to another's judgment rather than your own. Should this make you indifferent to paternalism? No. *Agnosticism* doesn't imply *indifference*.

Rejectability also risks regarding Joe's judgment of costs as no more his prerogative than that of the potential imposer. But it would be odd to think that Joe's judgment of costs and resulting beliefs and values does not come down to *his discretion*. Rejectability views do in fact recognize these worries to a limited extent. They forbid coercion based on matters the person himself regards as unacceptably costly, either in terms of performing some action or in gathering additional information on that action's relative merits. That's to say, Rejectability protects his evaluations about what he has *already* committed to rejecting, yet leaves up for grabs anything he has not yet considered in enough depth or at all. But his as-yet lack of commitment to considering alternative views is itself because of the sorts of costs discussed previously.

After the fact, Joe has taken the time to be in a position to reject some consideration – even if just to register his rejection without further explanation – while beforehand he has not taken the time (and may never) to be in a position to reject and merely not accept some consideration. So at best Rejectability seems arbitrarily fixed on the *past*. A defense of a person's judgment tailored to only his past judgments is ill-equipped to defend why it may override his possible future judgments.

If at R2 we considered it OK to interfere with you simply because you lacked reason to reject paternalism (but didn't have decisive reason to accept paternalism either), it sure seems like we are too quickly imposing a view on you. Not just paternalism: aren't there *many* other controversial views Rejectability would also allow us to impose on you too? "You lack decisive reason to reject immigration restrictions because you haven't been given a chance to consider their pros and cons? That's good enough – we'll pass a law restricting immigration!"

It's not OK to keep Middle People – those who neither accept nor reject CAD – from having the freedom to make bad choices since they aren't required to accept paternalism as the default view. It's at least legally OK for them to make bad choices because Acceptability is the preferable view on justifying coercive laws. But so far, I've assumed we're making free (enough) choices whether they're bad or not. What if lots of bad choices are also bad because they're not sufficiently free? We now turn to Chapter 5.

Five

What if CAD gets us nowhere in many situations because we are ensnared by biases that lead us astray – or we don't even know about our biases? That would be a rather hollow victory over *hard* paternalism if CAD is rarely applicable. We wouldn't merely face the costs discussed in the previous chapter. Rather, there would be biases that distort clear thinking and lead us to make faulty judgments all the time. Even if things aren't this bad, the distinction between hard and soft paternalism may be blurred because it's not always obvious when we are enough in control of our actions. Without a reliable way to distinguish the two, perhaps laws and regulations should err on the side of safety. Perhaps *soft* paternalism reigns supreme and justifies many laws and public policies that only seem hard paternalistic at first glance.

In this chapter, we'll look at cognitive and motivational biases that may detract from what a person really wants to do. What do I mean by a cognitive bias? Cognition refers to thought processes, and "bias" means a distorted representation of facts based on arbitrary factors that may keep you from believing or acting as you otherwise likely would in the absence of that distortion. This flaw could be because of something inherent in you – for instance, you might falsely think Vladimir Putin insists that you only eat ravioli. Or, it might be owing to lack of information – you think this is a bottle of root beer but it's actually poison. In either case your cognition is flawed, and soft paternalism might be called for because it's not really *you* making a free choice to do as you see fit based on the available facts. A motivational bias is somewhat connected to cognitive biases. Thinking and acting aren't two completely separate things, after all. I will treat motivational biases as the potential mistakes we make when attempting (or not attempting) to put a plan into action. Some biases will be a mix of the two, as I will outline.

In all cases, the question at hand is whether *choices might be bad because they're not really our own free choices.* We may then find soft paternalism to be justified at times even if we don't find hard paternalism to be justified. I will also discuss some ways in which nudges and other mild interventions may sometimes help us overcome our biases, or at least provide incentives to make better choices while preserving our freedom to make bad ones.

HOW IN CONTROL ARE WE?

Ben is a glutton who doesn't wear seat belts, smokes and drinks heavily, and is lazy. He lacks health insurance and spends all his disposable income on junk food and frivolous items that leave him empty. He considers himself a failure in prior attempts at projects because he dropped out of college and was fired from his previous jobs, and his hope of being a rock guitarist never materialized given his unwillingness to overcome his lack of manual dexterity. His past romantic relationships ended in disasters. He is apathetic because he also failed at prior half-hearted attempts to control his bad habits. He has alienated his friends, who now ignore him because they find his constant negative attitude draining, and so he is lonely, bored, depressed, even suicidal at times. He lost his motivation and sees any recovery as too hard an obstacle, and the potential loss of his unhealthy pleasures as a threat because he thinks they are all he has left. Moreover, Ben holds no CAD view – when asked about it he just chuckles sadly. It is difficult for him to understand the value of being in control of his life because he is "anhedonic" – finding no meaning or joy in anything – so he figures "why bother?"

Ben is a classic case of someone whom paternalism could potentially help enormously without major infringements of his freedom which, anyway, he is already undermining through his harmful choices. He has no appreciation of CAD as a defeater of paternalism, so why would it not be OK to interfere with him if it could at least light a fire under him by taking away options that constantly distract him from better paths? A critic may argue that all along I have been defending anti-paternalism for Gandhi or Socrates but not for average humans in a rut like Ben. Ideal cases of self-disciplined people are fine and good, the critique goes, but the matters which most motivate serious paternalists are concrete details about the lives of those who have cornered themselves, whose attitudes do not reflect an interest in free decisions to live well, who presumably have given up and place constant obstacles in front of whatever healthy pursuits they might have or once had. Such a person cannot merely "snap out of it". Maybe in these cases some soft paternalistic help is in order.

Sarah Conly argues that in many situations, people make bad choices not by their own fault but rather because they make errors in judgment. By letting them fail, we are not actually respecting their freedom because no truly free decision is being made. CAD may well be irrelevant in these situations, and the presumption is that we would want others to help us avoid these bad decisions even if our flawed current selves lack this desire. Moreover, simply appealing to persuasion may go nowhere. We might hear all the time that it's important to eat better, exercise, stop smoking, save more, and spend less – but then we go ahead and do the bad things with a deaf ear to good advice because it rings hollow compared with indulging in each present moment. It can be really hard to make better choices because it usually requires effort and a certain level of clearheaded thinking.

Conly's concerns are important. I grant that if a person lacks sufficient control over action A – or we don't have sufficient evidence that this person is in control of A – then it might be proper to interfere with a person doing A, even a known or prospective CADet, on the assumption that they are not freely choosing to do it. It may be a bad choice in large part because it's not their choice. We will consider some examples subsequently.

OUR MONKEY BRAINS

In this section, I will run through some biases and other psychological flaws. I hope to show that, even if these biases are sometimes detrimental, the important question is whether people are able to deal with them once alerted to their presence: no longer making bad choices, adoption of self-control strategies, or through consenting to aid. Ben may not be able to help himself much on his own since he doesn't know where to begin, but perhaps he is capable of asking for or accepting offers of assistance.

Having the humility to acknowledge your limitations and act on this wisdom is no small achievement. Knowing you are flawed allows you the responsibility to decide how you are going to handle things. Do you persist with making bad choices even with the knowledge that the choices might be because of cognitive errors? Instead, do you find ways to combat these errors so that you can make better choices? There might be room for soft paternalism if certain cognitive flaws to which we are blind prevent us from even being able to act in the ways that make freedom matter – especially if they encumber us from recognizing that we might need to seek or accept help. But how often are flaws this far-reaching? Are we forced to live in denial of them?

I will now survey some cognitive and motivational biases, suggesting where relevant when paternalism might be able to combat the negative effects of these errors while also indicating where relevant that otherwise competent people can and should freely accept this help rather than having it imposed on them. The silver lining is that knowledge of these flaws can allow us more self-awareness of our limits, and we can then plan around them without being subject to them unawares. As humans, we evolved as members of tribes. Our brains are still grappling with effective ways to handle the complexity of the large-scale cultures and institutions that were the product of our action but not of anyone's design. We are still wired to fear being eaten by tigers, and these days, some of us fear public speaking as much as tigers. By contrast, our brains are not exactly wired to fear the slow burn of running out of retirement money.

Affective Forecasting Errors

"Affect" is basically another word for emotions or feelings. People are often bad at predicting how they will feel in response to major, sometimes traumatic, changes.[1] Tragic loss of a limb or a beloved family member can of course be devastating, but we often underestimate our ability to adjust to the loss and overestimate the amount of time we will be overcome with heavy grief. These miscalculations might lead people to downplay their ability to cope with sickness or loss, causing the future to seem bleaker than it will be, and making them act more self-harmfully in the meantime.

Similarly, impact bias involves overestimation of positive or negative reactions to future events, and the related "hot-cold empathy gap" identifies human understanding as "state-dependent". For example, when one is angry, it is difficult to understand what it is like for one to be happy, and vice versa. Someone who just *has* to buy the fancy new TV, when their current one will do just fine for their purposes, might have distorted judgment in the heat of excitement over anticipating all the joy they might get from their new purchase . . . only to experience buyer's remorse on seeing that the new toy is not worth what was paid, when that money would have been better spent paying off their credit card balance. Impulse buys are made all the easier in today's world of instant online shopping. Rather than the costs of getting in the car and going to the big box store two towns over, people can indulge in Amazon Prime from their living rooms.

A defender of paternalism might claim that, where feasible, mandatory credit limits or "cooling off" periods would help, especially for items that people tend to regret buying or activities they regret doing in the heat of the moment. Without such enforced cooling off periods, people might not otherwise think twice before purchasing expensive luxuries since all they focus on is the excitement of the present moment, the future be damned. Again, would such interventions be instances of hard or soft paternalism?

But maybe we can help them through nudges instead of resorting to coercion, whether hard or soft paternalistic. A common practice when helping someone who might be making affective forecasting efforts is to ask them about previous times when they overestimated how sad or happy they would be. Prompting someone to think about these matters can aid him in keeping a perspective on what might otherwise not be on his mind. Relatedly, the "mere-measurement effect" describes how we can change a person's intentions merely by measuring, such as asking a question like "How likely are you to purchase a car?" Exposure to the question will often get someone to act more reflectively rather than impulsively while at the same time preserving the freedom to act impulsively.

Framing Effects

As discussed in Chapter 1, seemingly irrelevant factors can influence a person's choices differentially and so there are probably many situations where actual preferences predictably depart from true preferences, even if we cannot identify whether this is so in any given instance.[2] (Recall people who respond differently when told a surgery gives them a 9 in 10 chance of survival "versus" a 1 in 10 chance of dying.) Given scarce cognitive resources, it is not surprising that we use these heuristics. In Chapter 4, I discussed how the status-quo bias may often be helpful because it saves cognitive resources as people act on their default beliefs, and doing this is often rational unless the decision is important enough to consider alternatives based on their independent merits. Still, should a default opt-in option versus automatic enrollment into a 401(k) make such a big difference in people's behavior?

The related focusing illusion has to do with tunnel vision and failure to consider all relevant aspects of a problem, which might make sense in many cases if only some aspects of a problem need addressing. Still, these are blunt tools since the default is not always the best option and there may be some aspects that we overlook at our own peril.

So here paternalism may help by closing off immediate choices when certain alternatives warrant consideration, such as through bans or at least cooling-off periods. But there are alternative nudges too that allow people more freedom than mere bans: requiring them to choose whether to enroll or not enroll in a retirement account without either default option preselected, or announced default settings so people are aware of what's going on, or random framing of information (where possible), or full disclosure of information. For instance, a doctor might tell her patient: "This surgery has a 90% survival rate. It also has a 10% mortality rate. Just to be clear, those mean the same thing. You don't have to tell me now whether you want to have surgery. We can talk about it next week."

Framing biases may also be affected by what defenders of nudging call "choice architecture". This basically has to do with ways in which we can arrange an environment where someone is making decisions. For instance, people at a buffet tend to reach for food that's at eye level. A manager concerned with people making healthier nutritional choices might place salads and vegetables at eye level, while putting the cakes and cookies in a slightly harder to notice (or reach) part of the cafeteria. A significant number of people won't have strong preferences either way, so they will just put what's closest to them on their plates. However, those with stronger preferences for dessert will still have the option to get it, though they might have to work a bit harder than if the cakes were placed at eye level. This simple change to the choice architecture might have a profound influence in helping people make better choices, but at the same time the freedom of those with a sweet tooth is not being limited.

Confirmation Biases

Confirmation biases are cognitive and often take the form of wishful thinking: "it won't happen to me." People (even scientists!) often seek out information that confirms their prior beliefs without actively seeking disconfirming evidence or arguments. This also takes the form of optimism biases. Smokers, alcoholics, overeaters, and undersavers – insofar as they look out for relevant information – may tend to listen only to news stories or peers who are not terribly critical of their choices or comfort them that their decisions are normal and not unhealthy. They do not seek out contrary information, or they ignore it.

Since such people are resistant to seeking help or listening to good advice – after all, they might be in denial that they even need to seek help or advice – paternalism may better do the work they are unwilling to do. But a key question for this and other biases is whether refusal to seek or receive other evidence is largely uncontrollable, hence warranting soft not hard paternalism. When attention is called to your possibly bad choices, how do you react? Are you radically ignorant – that is, you don't even know that you might have a problem? Are you captive to uncorrectable biases?

One hypothesis: confirmation bias, wishful thinking, and self-deception are typically bugs we can control and change about ourselves, if *we choose*. We can identify times where we self-deceive and then try to arrange things for those future times, even if it can be hard. However, this is only an intuition on my part, and I don't want to rely on it. So, by contrast, people might not always be aware of their confirmation biases, or would have a very difficult time combating them even when given sufficient information, or their self-deception is beyond their conscious control in some cases. So perhaps here soft paternalism is relevant.

Another hypothesis: we have each other! John Stuart Mill gives a thought-provoking argument for a "community of speech and criticism" (my words) in Chapter 2 of *On Liberty*. On our own, we are quite prone to confirmation bias, but we *really* like pointing out each other's biases. Philosophers and scientists do this all the time, which is why they're so fun to have around at parties. But seriously, discussion and debate provide a "marketplace of ideas" and chances for us to learn from each other. We are not isolated atoms – our language is public and our knowledge is a matter of collaboration. We learn from others' mistakes too. Can you think of times when you've seen someone stubbornly making the same bad choices over and over and told yourself "I am not going to be that person"?

Availability Biases

With this cognitive bias, remote and extreme recent events are often exaggerated, while less "scary" risks are underappreciated for the level of harm they pose. Many people are terrified of earthquakes or plane crashes and alter their behavior out of proportion to the risk – they buy earthquake insurance in areas where risks are minimal, or they stop flying and drive more, actually increasing their odds of being in a fatal accident since driving is more dangerous than flying. Meanwhile, some of these same people who are excessively risk-averse toward planes and earthquakes also engage in far riskier activities – smoking or overeating or failing to have health insurance. The dangers of such activities are typically less vivid and dramatic. They don't often make headline news ("if it bleeds, it leads"). In a way, people's differential behavior makes sense. Plane crashes are horrific even though they are extremely rare, while slowly expanding waistlines are often not frightening enough to motivate corrective action. For mundane harms there is no clock ticking off extra days of one's life being lost, so the harms are hard to appreciate in the abstract.

Nudges such as images of cancerous lungs or an empty bank account when one is elderly may provide some needed vividness but might not move people affected by the confirmation biases or wishful thinking mentioned earlier. Many people do not think of themselves as getting lung cancer or being impoverished after retirement age – that's someone else's problem. Interestingly though, smokers tend to overestimate, relative to nonsmokers, the average years of life that smoking cuts short. This may suggest that if the very people most exposed to health risks often exaggerate those risks yet continue to smoke, they may well be expressing strong preferences in favor of the habit!

Conly suggests that people's failure to wear seat belts or quit smoking may be because of an inability to appreciate the hard-to-envision trauma that could visit them. If so, maybe coercion is in order, or maybe people should be free to go their merry ways. Does an inability to imaginatively rehearse danger on a gut level detract from one's ability to make better decisions? Do we need more vividness or will some people still make bad(?) choices regardless? Perhaps if vividness doesn't really work, reminders and the mere-measurement effect could have more impact. Asking a person how long they plan to continue smoking, or how long they plan to wait before opening a retirement account, could prompt them to make better choices – by their own lights – in ways that mere imagery does not.

Decision Fatigue

Making decisions for oneself (even those one enjoys making) and resisting temptations deplete one's resources for self-control, which affects motivation.[3] We are less likely to make silly mistakes in the morning when we have more energy, but we grow wearier and more distractible as the day goes on. Moreover, we often confront situations with "too much choice" where fewer options would not overwhelm us and allow us to make better choices on our own terms. If it's hard enough to choose among nineteen different brands and varieties of deodorant, imagine having to choose a retirement account or health insurance plan among a lot of varieties, each with its own set of policies and stipulations. Studies have shown that online daters go for a far smaller percentage of people whose profiles they look at, whereas speed-dating with fewer options yields higher dating rates. Constraints may help one make good choices rather than putting off choice indefinitely.

Barry Schwartz and his colleagues have conducted studies that show adoption of a "satisficing" attitude, where one selects an option deemed "good enough", often brings more satisfaction and less anxiety than a "maximizing" attitude, where the person feels compelled to undertake the often costly exercise of surveying all available options to find the best one, and then thereafter second guesses and

Why It's OK to Make Bad Choices

laments the possibility that maybe he neglected the best option.[4] Standard accounts of rationality posit that rational agents always maximize the choices in their available option set, but there is nothing inherently valuable about choice as such – only choice as it contributes to a valuable goal, habit, activity, or relationship. Given the search costs (among other costs) discussed in Chapter 4, trying to find the best is often costlier overall – in terms of expended resources and stress – than "settling" for the sufficiently good and ending one's search there. (Do not tell your partner if this is how you chose them.)

Conceptions like CAD might assume that choice is some kind of limitless resource when in fact people are in need of paternalism when they are exhausted by too much of it. As Conly discusses, taking away some of their decisions might free them to make the kinds of choices that matter most in their lives while relieving them of the burden of more mundane albeit important decisions. A big question for present purposes – is maximizing an uncorrectable attitude that entraps some, or can people become satisficers by changing their mental habits without undue effort? Or, at least, knowing that they are maximizers and that this gets them into trouble sometimes, can they arrange choice-limiting situations voluntarily?

Online retailers such as Amazon could offer helpful nudges here. One could commit to only purchasing the highest-rated of a given item rather than getting overwhelmed at a physical store by all the brand varieties. This "crowdsourcing" of shopping could allow maximizers to rest assured that they're probably getting among the best of a given brand without having to try out everything themselves. Nudges like these can make choice less overwhelming to consumers.

Addiction

Drug dependence like addiction is both a cognitive and motivational effect. It often leaves users with much lower tendencies to project into the future. One study showed that drug addicts asked to fill in the details of a story projected on average only nine days into the future compared with four years for non-addicts.[5] There is debate in the psychology literature whether mental disease or bad habit best explains addictive tendencies. We can't get into that enormous debate here other than to note that people's theories of addiction will lead them to have different views on how much free choice the addict really has over his actions. A habit model suggests that addicts are capable of breaking their addictions by developing different, replacement habits. A disease model suggests that addicts lack much ability to do even this – claiming they can overcome their addiction through better choices is like saying to a cancer patient that he can cure his disease through better choices. Some long-term addictions to narcotics and opioids may even be physical and require medical not just psychological treatment.

There is also much debate over the best forms of treatment for addiction: cognitive behavioral therapy, aversion therapy, certain medicines, 12-step programs, etc. Different treatments may work better or worse depending on the individual and his circumstances. Whatever the case, banning or restricting the availability of certain addictive substances might motivate people who would otherwise mire themselves in addiction and thus never shed the extreme short-termism needed to recover. However, we should note that whatever your view on addiction, the addiction itself need not make one incapable of recognizing that one needs help or listening to others when they suggest as much.

Perhaps even the low-functioning addict still has feedback (lost job, poor health, broken relationships, lost money, etc.) that suggests his life may not be going very well and maybe he can take a step to address it. Even if addiction is a disease that the addict can't cure directly, it doesn't mean that the disease keeps the addict from being able to seek or accept help, any more than cancer keeps a cancer patient from being able to seek or accept help. But even if there is no room at all for choice in many cases of addiction, that only shows that CAD would not be *relevant* in such cases, not that CAD is *false*. Our interventions with addicts would then be soft paternalistic.

Procrastination

Procrastination is a motivational issue. Almost all of us procrastinate some of the time. (The author procrastinated a bit on writing this section.) This habit involves avoidance of doing a task which one acknowledges needs to be accomplished – not merely delaying an action with an intention to do it later; rather, delaying the execution of an action one intends to perform, often with excuses like "I don't feel like doing this now" or "it can wait a little longer." It is the practice of doing more pleasurable things in place of less pleasurable ones, or carrying out less urgent tasks instead of more urgent ones, thus putting off impending tasks to a later time.

Procrastination is above all a self-control problem with various sources. One source is mood regulation – it temporarily relieves us of having to choose responsibly, but later comes back to haunt us when we feel worse about matters left undone than if we had not procrastinated. Procrastination can also stem from task aversion.[6] Tasks that are frustrating, boring, or resented unsurprisingly generate the most procrastination. (These issues do *not* apply to my writing of this book.) Procrastination can also be explained by time fragmentation in which people make decisions that might be rational at a given moment but are additively irrational.[7] "This one cigarette won't harm me," the smoker tells himself, but he makes that isolated assessment for each cigarette, so while the negligible adds up to a lot in reality, the smoker only focuses on the negligible at each self-contained episode and doesn't appreciate the additive nature of his habit. At each moment, we don't necessarily have a view to the aggregated long run.

Procrastination also stems from threat avoidance. One study showed that heavy procrastinators actually turned in an assignment sooner than light procrastinators when the threat of social "exposure" was low.[8] This surprising result could suggest that heavy procrastinators are often driven by external motivations like fear of social disapproval, so they will prioritize the "easy" things whereas the less fearful light procrastinators will order tasks according to factors other than increasing threat level. Procrastinators are more likely to avoid tasks where the odds of success are uncertain, and often rationalize their avoidance by telling themselves: "It wasn't really that important anyway."

Could nudges such as commitment devices work? A commitment device is a choice you make in the present that restricts the choices you can make in the future. Consider "peer accountability", for instance. You announce to your friend that you will give him 100 dollars if you don't lose 10 pounds in the next two months – trust me, your friend will suddenly be interested in holding you accountable![9] Websites such as StickK offer opportunities for people to make public commitment contracts and select a referee to hold them accountable in trying to reach their goals. For instance, if a staunch Democrat is trying to lose weight, they might make a commitment to donate money to a rival organization (such as the Republican Party) if the goals are not met. These kinds of incentives can work wonders when people are trying to avoid having to do something that they strongly dislike.

Maybe commitment devices often won't work for all procrastinators, however, because some will simply put off initiating *that* precommitment too. Procrastination even for seeking help or establishing commitment devices suggests a place for hard paternalism – where feasible, banning the sorts of distractions and temptations that commonly lead people to procrastinate, or requiring retirement savings and purchase of health insurance rather than relying on people who never get around to it.

On the other hand, procrastination still seems like a choice within a person's control. Therapists recommend that an effective way to battle avoidance tactics is, to recall the Nike slogan, "Just do it." Stop thinking about it, stop hesitating, hold your nose and just get it done. It's probably not as bad as you fear (recall affective forecasting errors), and you'll be relieved and happier in the long run. Choosing to procrastinate just feeds anxiety as tasks build up that avoidance won't magically make disappear.

Dunning-Kruger Effect

This effect is a cognitive matter and involves a failure in non-experts of knowing that one doesn't know much about a particular matter.[10] Poorer performers often overestimate their ability at some task while expert performers tend to sell themselves short. Poorer performers are often overconfident because they aren't good enough to know how difficult the tasks are – they can't assess themselves in light of fuller information about what's possible and how they fall short. They face radical ignorance or "unknown unknowns" about their abilities relative to certain tasks or subjects. People who are not experts in medicine or statistics might fancy themselves more competent than those experts to decide whether to take risky drugs or buckle up. They may underestimate the risks owing to sheer ignorance. Belief perseverance experiments show that many people refuse to update their mistaken beliefs even when confronted with clear arguments or evidence that these beliefs are wrong.[11]

Here paternalism, where feasible, might involve seat belt laws or the requirement for certain drugs to be prescribed by doctors only. People who, say, pursue homeopathic remedies with the stubborn insistence that they work might benefit from being forbidden from pursuing quack medicine in the first place. Again, the question of whether this involves soft or hard paternalism turns on whether people have or lack sufficient control over their ignorance. Can they at least suck it up and admit that they might lack good reason to be confident in their beliefs, especially when someone shows them that they are wrong? If that's really hard for someone to do, is it because they *can't help* but keep believing false things, or is it because they're not *willing* to question their beliefs when confronted?

Nudges might work here as well. A person suffering the Dunning-Kruger effect might be prompted to think of times when they were wrong before but had insisted that they were right. Or, if they want to make a sincere effort to test their beliefs, they can try to think of the best argument that opposes their view. Such intellectual humility can often lead people to become less confident of false beliefs that they once hold with more insistence.

Misregulation is a cognitive matter and involves the mistaken belief that X will lift one's mood when doing X will in fact make one's mood worse.[12] A classic example is binge drinking. A person might feel a nice buzz after a couple drinks and tell herself that the best way to maintain that good feeling is to keep pounding back cocktails. There comes a point on one's blood-alcohol level where euphoria ebbs and unhappiness increases with subsequent drinks, but the drunk person is often a poor judge of when this line is being crossed and so keeps going. Paternalism could involve restrictions on how much alcohol or other legal but risky substances can be sold to a person at a given time. For those who go on shopping or gambling binges, perhaps there can be restrictions on what they can charge to their credit cards during a given time span.[13] People who might be tempted to fire off an angry message could benefit from software that delays their e-mails or text messages briefly when suspicious keywords show unproductive rage – allowing them to cool down and reconsider.

Are people incapable of avoiding misregulation? Perhaps the buzzed person is still able to *choose* to cut himself off. Or, if he can't trust his willpower to resist temptation, he can ask the bartender ahead of time to cut him off after a certain number of drinks, or hand over his wallet to a friend (hopefully not a stranger). If his drinking has become enough of a problem that even these measures don't help, he can take the radical step of not going to bars and maybe instead going to therapy, until his dependence is under his control. *That* decision at least is under his control.

Licensing Effect

This effect is cognitive and motivational and involves acting as if one good deed (say, exercising) gives one permission to make bad choices afterward.[14] In fact, simply thinking about doing good often allows one the excuse to do bad. As a result, arming consumers with health information may be necessary for them to make informed decisions, but it is far from sufficient.[15] Interestingly, people with more self-control actually fare worse when healthier options are introduced to an otherwise unhealthy menu. They might avoid a purely unhealthy menu, but irrelevant alternatives to healthy options lead them to choose the bad alternatives. *Feeling* that one has worked harder (even when one hasn't) makes one feel hungrier and more likely to indulge, a phenomenon known as "justification without ego depletion".[16]

These examples indicate interesting ways in which people who might otherwise be relatively good at pursuing their ends are sometimes subject to effects which show up more negatively in them than in their less goal-oriented or disciplined counterparts. They may vindicate Conly's argument that paternalism is aptly directed at all of us, not merely some alleged "underclass" of foolish sinners who need elites to control them. The evidence also suggests that bans might be more effective than informational nudges for dealing with licensing effects since informational nudges could have the opposite effect of their intended consequences.

Maybe there's an alternative to paternalism since the more we know about licensing effects in ourselves, the more we may be able to do something about them! How? Maybe ignore calorie postings and make a rule for yourself: "Don't eat if you don't feel the slightest bit hungry." People tend to be better at following rules than doing math anyway, so giving yourself commands can have its benefits. Whatever the case, I care in this book about *free* choice that reflects your ability to control what you do.

HARD VERSUS SOFT PATERNALISM: HOW CAN WE TELL THE DIFFERENCE?

What do these biases and flaws have in common with regard to paternalism? Are people so overcome by them that they systematically fail at their own goals while also being unaware that the biases are in effect or are unable to control their negative effects? Sometimes people are going to make mistakes, take ineffective means toward their goals, not reach their most preferred outcomes, etc. The question is whether these flaws often imply helplessness in certain instances, or whether, aware of the possibility of error and bad consequences, people retain the ability to decide what to do about their potentially bad choices, even if the best decision sometimes involves consenting to another's oversight or treatment.

What about cases in which *we don't know* whether a person is acting in control when they make bad choices? Is it sometimes OK to stop them so we can figure out what's going on? That seems plausible. My sense is that people would be more open to the following rationale: "We are interfering with you because we don't know whether you are in control of your actions right now." Even if the person turns out to be in control – and let's say they're a CADet too – the interference may still be justified to the CADet even though it frustrates their ability to act freely in that moment. What seems much harder to justify is the following rationale: "We are interfering with you *even though* we are confident that you are in control of your actions right now." Does this distinction make sense? If so, it might also suggest why private interventions are generally preferable to laws and regulations. People closest to me, or those who have a lot of information about me, are likely to be better at making this distinction.

But are private interventions only limited to *soft* paternalism? I don't think so. Remember Hanna's example of Reckless Hiker, the guy who knows a bridge he is about to cross *may* be deadly, but who decides to cross anyway. Sure, he doesn't want to die, but it's not clear whether he would want me to stop him from crossing when I know the bridge is deadly. I can't help thinking, however, that in almost all cases he would want me to stop him if I didn't have time to warn him. But let's say I stop him and the ungrateful twerp reacts as follows: "How dare you keep me from crossing! How do you know I didn't really want to die, or at least didn't want the freedom to make a very bad choice?" I feel like I would be entirely reasonable to respond: "Look, I don't have that information about you, but I know this much: if you had crossed, I'd have to watch you die, knowing I could have done something to stop you temporarily. So next time wear a shirt that reads something like 'Don't Stop Me From Crossing Bad Bridges' and then I'll know to leave you alone."

Perhaps a single sentence to summarize the thesis of this chapter is: if part of what makes a choice bad is that it's unfree, then it's not the kind of choice that *matters*.

Six

In this chapter I will explore whether it's not OK to make bad choices if they impose undue costs on society.

Remember Football Fred? He's gained a few pounds since you first read about him, but he still enjoys feasting on sodas and junk food after having retired from his professional athletic career. He now leads a low-energy life devoted to binge-watching his favorite television shows and is obese as a result. Jen enjoys rock climbing, cross-fit training, and salads. Some would contend that Fred's liberty to engage in his unhealthy lifestyle is more appropriately subject to potential legal restriction than are Jen's chosen activities. One argument is that Jen's way of living is more valuable than Fred's. She is making something of herself, whereas he is now wasting away his retirement days and hurting his health. While there may be something to this argument, I will put it aside for two reasons.

First, in a liberal democracy, it is uncomfortable at best to pass judgments − at least if one thinks they should be *legally enforced* − on the value of what free and equal people reveal themselves to prefer. We might implore, chide, shame, or otherwise suggest that people we take to be making bad choices should consider changing their ways. Beyond that, reliance on law smacks of "political perfectionism", the view that the state can make value judgments about the worth of various ways of life in determining what laws to pass.[1] Most liberal views reject political perfectionism and hold that the state should not take an official position on which ways of life are better or worse, provided these ways of life don't cause others great harm or violate their rights.

Second, even if Fred's preferences are for objectively less worthwhile actions, or "lower" pleasures, he may also value having the freedom to engage in behaviors that are themselves non-valuable or downright self-harmful. He may be a CADet, that is. If we understand this freedom as an element of a person's life philosophy, denying Fred this freedom not only frustrates his ability to live as he sees fit, it imposes a view on him that he needn't hold, as was discussed in Chapters 3 and 4.

However, paternalistic rationales are not the only ones relevant to the question of whether people's liberties should be restricted sometimes. There is also the question of whether some liberties risk imposing unfair social costs *on others*. Neither Fred nor Jen are islands – their actions don't affect only themselves – and we can't assume that they do or should absorb the full costs of their actions were they to be seriously harmed from their choices. That is, they may have claims on us that we cannot or should not avoid. Fred may end up in the emergency room after making lots of bad dietary choices, he may raise our insurance rates, and our taxes may end up paying for much of his care. (We'll leave aside that Fred is a retired pro athlete and so should be able to afford his own care.) Is it fair for us responsible people to pay for those who may have acted irresponsibly?

Consider what I will call the "Principle of Beneficence" (PB): **Citizens have a legally enforceable duty to help even those sick or injured people who choose to risk suffering severe self-imposed harm by their actions and are unable**

Why It's OK to Make Bad Choices

to care for themselves or afford their treatment. Because this duty may impose significant social costs, we may be justified in restricting people's liberty to engage in certain risky behaviors, not for paternalistic reasons, but to prevent us from having to incur the costs of helping those in dire need after the fact. Their choices are bad because they harm us – and that may not be OK at all!

I will not argue for PB but will assume it's plausible. Fred or Jen would presumably *welcome* our aid post-injury if they were unable to afford the costs of treatment, and it would be out of the question for (say) hospitals to refuse treatment if people were seriously injured and could not afford it. Imagine you're a doctor and Jen is bleeding in the hospital parking lot – do you shake your head and tell her she can't come in because she is uninsured and her bank account isn't large enough? However, PB leads to the possibility of higher taxes and higher premiums within insurance pools and greater consumption of health resources. Some might object that they are unfairly burdened by others' decisions, and they should not have to pay for other people's unwise or risky choices. They have a point. (You know that feeling when you order the cheapest item on the menu while the rest of your group goes wild, and then some genius decides everyone should split the bill equally so you end up subsidizing other people's dinners? Pretty annoying, right? Maybe the same issue applies here to those who suck up medical resources on our dime. Did they stop to consider how their actions could hurt *us*?)

Moreover, if we lower the cost of risky decisions, we can expect more risky decisions from people who anticipate that they will not have to absorb the full costs of their actions. (Compare this with the behavior of big banks, who often continue to make high-risk loans with the expectation that they will be bailed out if the financial bubble bursts.) In light of PB, the objection goes, we should restrict certain risky liberties to prevent unfairly burdening those who were not responsible for the harms' coming about.

Questions remain as to whether this objection is decisive. It may be natural to think that, in light of social costs, Jen should still be free to rock climb whereas Fred's liberty to drink sodas, smoke, or eat junk food is properly subject to restriction if not outright prohibition. But this raises the question of why, if social costs are the main concern of PB, we should assume restriction of Fred's liberties is acceptable but not Jen's liberty to rock climb. After all, it is an open question as to which kinds of activities and behavior tend to generate net social costs over a person's lifetime. In fact, some studies have shown strong evidence that smokers actually pay more into the health care system than they receive – while in a given year they cost more, overall they are net providers given their shorter average life spans.[2] (Yes, that's a bit morbid . . . but it's true.) Studies on obesity have shown that it's inconclusive whether the obese are net providers for similar reasons, but it's not at all clear that they are net burdens.

On the other hand, typically accepted liberties might impose net overall costs on the rest of us. Jen might fall from a rock and become paralyzed, needing constant expensive care for many years. Instead, she might avoid injury and be so healthy from the exercise that she lives a very long life and ends up taking more from the public budget (Social Security, Medicare) than she contributes. Any liberty could be potentially at risk of restriction if *social costs* are the primary concern motivating talk of restricting liberties. Singling out some liberties, particularly those which do not in fact generate net social costs – like smoking and overeating – invites charges of discrimination.

So, in light of PB, we face the following conundrum. Either (1) we restrict or prohibit perhaps a significant number of socially costly liberties some people might nonetheless find important or meaningful, risking a rather authoritarian setting; (2) we privilege certain liberties on grounds other than their expected social costliness, risking a rather arbitrary setting; or (3) we allow some people to free ride when they cannot afford care for severe self-imposed harms. None of this sounds appealing, so is there a way around this three-horned problem?

My hunch is that mandatory insurance, which I will defend later, offers a potential solution. Before defending this scheme, I will briefly highlight four possible but inadequate responses to the prior concerns. The first is what I call the "strongly cold-hearted" response, which in effect denies PB. This view holds that people should be free to harm themselves in whatever way they choose, but they have no legal (and perhaps no moral) claim on us afterward if in fact they meet with even severe harms they cannot afford to treat. They are on their own after assuming such a risk because it was their responsibility, and any aid they receive from us is a voluntary act of charity rather than an enforceable duty.

It is doubtful many would prefer this response upon reflection. A duty of beneficence reflects concern for a person's well-being even if they are largely to blame for causing the harm they undergo. By contrast, a view that allows us to look a suffering fellow person in the eye and deny them help at no unreasonable cost to ourselves is hardly consistent with the respect and concern that is part of liberal morality. Telling someone "too bad – you are responsible for your choices" is fine in many contexts, but not in one that is a matter of life and limb. Now some libertarians out there may disagree, and maybe you're right, but how would you go about convincing someone who thinks PB is true?

The second response I call "weakly coldhearted", wherein people who want the freedom to harm themselves can give informed consent to opt out of receiving public aid for future harm incurred, and they have no claim on us afterward if they, in fact, harm themselves. For instance, Fred may acknowledge the harms of obesity in a signed letter that is a matter of public record, which can reassure us that he is not unwittingly assuming risks. His future risks of harm are "known unknowns", to borrow a phrase from former Secretary of Defense Donald Rumsfeld. That is, he is aware that what he does is risky (a "known"), unlike young children or the unaware pedestrian in Mill's unsafe bridge example who are not even aware of risks. What remains unknown is whether in fact his risky choices will bring him harm or what the nature and severity of any such harm might be.

This response is also unsatisfying, however, mainly because beneficence may not be the kind of duty that is conditional or contractually waivable. Also, people often have optimism biases that blind them to the full force of the risks they undertake. A person might cheerfully sign away his claim to aid when times are good, but then desperately want that aid when severely harmed. Skeptics might use the same move against the weakly coldhearted view that I use against paternalists – they could hold that it's unclear whether the rights-waiver guy is informed in a vivid enough sense of the risks he is taking, or whether he is merely engaging in cheap talk to get away with doing what he wants to do at the time. Moreover, this claim carries a force that his prior consent to waive may not overcome. We still have the problem of future Fred suffering a lot *regardless* of whether he acknowledged the risks beforehand,

and this acknowledgment makes it no less difficult to turn him away from our aid. Perhaps this approach works for relatively minor harms such as gout from overeating. Gout is painful but not necessarily debilitating, but what if the future harm is a massive stroke?

The third response I call "having it all" – people should be free to engage in risky activities, and sometimes they will have a claim on us afterward if harm comes that they can't afford to treat. That is simply the price of liberty coupled with moral duties, whether beneficence or some other kind. That we might find these duties socially costly at times is not an argument against either liberty or the duties, since all obligations are costly to some degree. To enjoy the benefits of associating with each other in a liberal democracy we must also bear some burdens. We may have to pull over for ambulances, pay taxes, serve on juries, or catch colds from others. I don't have a right to take a shortcut to my house, trampling my neighbor's garden in the process, since she has a property right over her front lawn. The sometimes high costs of respecting property rights are no argument against the importance of such, and the "having it all" response applies the same lesson to rights involving one's choice of preferred activity.

While this view has some merit, at some point we still need to weigh liberty considerations against social cost considerations. Liberty cannot always win because at some point liberty might allow people to engage in unacceptably costly actions to others – costs that, in fact, themselves significantly impede other people's liberties to use resources that are otherwise being taxed away to pay for the injured. Again, it is an open question just how high social costs might be. But a view that defends all liberties as having *infinite* weight over other considerations is committed to claiming that no intended self-regarding action, however otherwise costly to society, should be prohibited, which is probably not a conclusion one wants to be stuck holding.

The final, "restrictive" response is closest to the policies we see currently in place. This response maintains that some actions lack enough socially recognized importance and need to be restricted to prevent costly beneficence duties. The way we determine which liberties are not protected is to assess the importance (objective or subjective) of the activities at hand. A clear case of differential treatment might involve protecting Jen's liberty to rock climb if this activity plays a key role in her life, whereas we might restrict Fred's liberty to drink sodas and eat giant portions of fried food since these are not necessarily items he would deeply miss in the long run if they were prohibited. Giant helpings of soda and potato chips do not play a major role in the development of his talents and interests even if they satisfy the cravings of his reptile brain, and after intervention his preferences can change toward healthier pursuits.[3]

Nonetheless, this response is unsatisfying too because it brings us back to the worry about how we get to decide the worth of different liberties, and who gets to decide. Some people (like Football Fred) might strongly enjoy fatty food as a significant part of their lives. Gluttony may be a sin for some but not for them. Others might be CADets who want the freedom to make bad choices. Even if Fred does *not* have strong preferences to engage in his unhealthy behavior as such, we cannot assume that he also would lack any good reason to endorse the freedom to make such choices. The "restrictive" response threatens to stray from social cost considerations into making controversial judgments about the worth of liberties, or the shape of their ethical codes, to people who might differ considerably from each other about what matters in their lives.

Why It's OK to Make Bad Choices

We want to avoid a "tyranny of the majority". If being in the majority is all we need to confer legitimacy on a law, then any number of horrible decisions could oppress people with minority views. That's why we have a liberal democracy. We need liberal rights to serve as bulwarks against tyrannical majorities. But if my arguments work, a right against restrictions of one's conception of the good has strong if not decisive force against majority opinion.

THE COASE IS CLEAR?

So far, we have viewed the matter of social costs largely through the lens of outright prohibitions, but perhaps those are needlessly blunt tools. I would like to consider an alternative approach, somewhat akin to what economists call a "Coasean bargain". Roughly speaking, the Coase Theorem concerns whether and how we can compensate "losers" when property rights come into conflict. These are matters of "negative externalities". For example, a new airport leads to airplane noise invading the homes of nearby residents. If they have some kind of legitimate claim to a quieter living area, perhaps the airlines should be required to pay for the residents' soundproof windows. An aspect of the Coasean approach can often involve a bargain to determine who is willing to accept restriction of liberties or who is willing to pay for allowance of liberties.

Imagine that liberty of action is the default – people are free to act how they please, even if doing so subjects others to social costs. One way of dissuading people from engaging in actions that generate socially costly externalities is to pay them not to engage in those actions. If our concern is the net lifetime health-care costs people like Joe may generate, one option is to offer him sufficient payment not to make these costly choices. This approach has the virtue of avoiding coercion since the offer is Joe's to take or leave.

This seems like a cool idea that will work sometimes. However, the offer to pay suffers from three problems. First, bluffers could easily take advantage of the offer by threatening to engage in risky activities that they would never actually perform. This could lead to an even larger transfer of wealth than the taxation PB might generate, not to mention compliance costs associated with monitoring whether people are honoring their agreements. There is also a greater chance such people would cheat on their agreement since they are motivated by the external incentive of money rather than an internal motivation to form healthier habits.

Second, there may be people who would still not accept the highest realistic offer to quit since they have the option to refuse. Demand for hard drugs is often highly inelastic, for instance. This just means that increases in the price of a drug often do not lead users to lower how much they use. If the price of spaghetti tripled, lots of people would cut down on how much spaghetti they buy, or they would substitute something cheaper like Ramen noodles. Drugs are different especially if people are highly dependent on them. So those who value using drugs strongly enough, including addicts, may refuse any realistic offers, which still leaves us with enforceable beneficence duties should harm befall anyone.

Finally, even if we could avoid the first two matters, it is still unclear whether it would be just as, if not more, costly to pay people than it would be simply to enforce either a scheme of prohibitions (the "restrictive" view) or widespread liberties coupled with taxation to help the unfortunate (the "having it all" view).

Maybe all hope is not lost though. Consider a reverse situation where *restriction* of socially costly liberties is the default and people who value this or that liberty can purchase the right to engage in it. Joe can buy the freedom to use drugs (perhaps through paying a sales tax) and Jen can buy the freedom to rock climb (perhaps through purchasing insurance). The revenue from taxes or mandatory insurance can go to a fund that pays for the aid of those who are badly harmed by the behaviors in question and who cannot afford treatment. This approach may avoid the discrimination worry since restriction is based on only social cost considerations rather than controversial views about the importance of a particular liberty. It is also more efficient since people can reflect how much they value certain freedoms through their willingness to pay for them. Of course, one worries that default restriction of many liberties may not be a characteristic we'd want a liberal democracy to have. I must leave aside that concern for now.

MANDATORY INSURANCE?

Perhaps a mandatory insurance scheme would be the most effective way of protecting people's liberties by providing assurance that liberties will not be subject to prohibition owing to the risk of social costs. It might be socially efficient to force people into insurance pools where they share some costs and benefits over long periods of time, and where any new inefficiencies this raises can be partially reduced by co-payments, deductibles, and premiums.[4] Although treating restriction as a default may run afoul of liberal sensibilities, where typically there is a presumption in favor of liberties, many in the liberal tradition regard some liberties as potentially subject to restriction if that can bring about large social gains. One virtue of being able to purchase the right to engage in a particular liberty is that one is not subject to heavy-handed prohibitions.

Another worry may lurk, however, about people who cannot afford enough insurance to cover many of their desired liberties. People who may already be among the worst off could face the further burden (and insult?) of being denied the ability to engage in risky activities that more privileged individuals can do. Jen might be denied the freedom to rock climb, and Joe might be denied the freedom to play hockey, if both are unable to afford the possibly higher insurance premiums covering such activities. The concern is that our liberal democracy may end up looking more feudalistic than liberal, where privileged classes can buy more freedom while worse-off classes are denied the chance not merely by lamentable unintended circumstances but *by law*.

Rich people telling poor people what they can and can't do is not a feature of *liberal* societies. This state of affairs comes uncomfortably close to denying the equal moral status of all members – a steep price to pay compared with social cost concerns. Unlike democratic prohibition of a liberty, where the body politic subjects the entirety of its members to the same prohibition, leaving all on equal footing with regard to the ban, this arrangement grants some people legal freedom denied to others based simply on ability to pay.

There may be a way around this problem. Rather than assume everyone must contribute a fixed amount to the insurance pool, a sliding scale that accounts for ability to pay might work.[5] The idea is that a bunch of uninsured people engaging in risky behavior is more of a burden than requiring everyone to pay what they can for the restrictions they want lifted. The poorest may pay lower premiums, or none at all, for liberties they want to have. Those in higher brackets, who tend to benefit *disproportionately* – if not unjustly – from liberal institutions, would pay higher premiums (or perhaps higher co-payments or deductibles) for liberties *they* want to have, as needed to cover everyone in the pool. This approach is almost certainly not a cure-all, if anything can be. The better-off may have to pay more, in addition to whatever freedoms they wish to cover, so as to help subsidize the worse-off.[6]

Some might find this objectionable. Let's say we end up with a weird result where the worst-off want all the risky freedoms and the better-off don't. Does that just bring us back to the social costs question? Or is it the case that the better-off can't complain about paying for the worse-off because not all wealthy people's money is theirs by merit? My best answer, and it may be disappointing, is that there are no panaceas. It remains unclear what a better alternative would be if: (1) we seek to let everyone have as much freedom as they want all else being equal, (2) we acknowledge PB, (3) we look to avoid arbitrary restriction of liberties, and (4) we seek the most cost-efficient policies consistent with these three items. Mandating insurance means that at-risk people of whatever income or wealth level would pay what they can into the pool, which may be more cost-effective than if uninsured free riders could benefit from a system into which they contributed nothing.[7]

In the absence of clear evidence for many cases, it remains unclear whether social costs apply to a broad range of freedoms. If they do apply, however, then concerns about cost, not paternalism, are possible rationales for restriction of certain liberties. However, ability to pay should not be an obstacle for those who value what might be socially costly liberties. For a liberal democracy to avoid discrimination and inequality, people should have the right to buy their freedom across any domain, and inability to pay should not be an obstacle. A mandatory insurance scheme with a sliding-scale payment structure is one proposal to consider if restriction of socially costly liberties is the default.

I'll stop there as I've probably managed to anger everyone at some point in this chapter. Things are complicated – don't shoot the messenger! If anything, though, I hope to have suggested ways in which it's OK to make bad choices *if allowing them doesn't place undue costs on others*.

Why We Should Be Careful

Seven

So, have I convinced you that people should be *free* to do pretty much whatever they want to themselves even if they shouldn't? It's OK if you're still not persuaded since that probably means you've been giving the matter a lot of thought. There are words other than final ones, and I can't pretend to have given a complete and knockdown set of arguments. But even if you still think paternalism is fine in a lot of cases, I'll make one more appeal that asks you to consider whether paternalistic laws will capture the aims that their defenders intend. It's one thing to craft legislation that works in theory, but that can be an odd assumption when defenders of legal paternalism start with the very observation that we humans are far from perfect.

Sure, there are ways in which we can work together, can form institutions under the right conditions that largely correct for the kinds of errors and biases we otherwise face as individuals. (Recall from Chapter 5 how a "marketplace of ideas" can help us check each other's confirmation biases.) However, it's odd to motivate the discussion of paternalism by pointing out our imperfections as private actors without paying at least as much attention to how people's imperfections as public actors may play out when trying to implement paternalistic laws and policies. In this chapter, I will look at two problems with such laws and policies: the bad incentives that prohibition often fosters, and the unintended consequences of many regulations. Thus, *it may be OK to have the freedom to make bad choices if the costs of trying to restrict them outweigh the benefits.*

BAD INCENTIVES: THE DARK SIDE OF PROHIBITION

Prohibitions can run into all kinds of problems even if they are good in theory. After all, if we ban something bad, there should be less of it, right? End of story. But in theory, we can all make better choices too – that we don't motivates the case for hard paternalism in the first place. As a matter of fact, we don't make better choices, but theory says we can if we tried. So why prohibit at all – why shouldn't all of us just make more effort to choose wisely when we can? If the response is "But we don't make that effort", we should be sure to see if the implementation of paternalistic laws runs into similar problems. Can we assume that flawed people will use laws wisely enough to correct for their lack of wisdom? Maybe so, but it's not obvious.

That prohibitions can raise problems is an understatement if we examine U.S. alcohol prohibition from the 1920s or the more recent War on Drugs. Consider our current prohibition of many types of narcotics. If people want a particular illegal drug badly enough, they will often resort to black markets, which can be rife with violence and corruption. Illegal heroin bought from a criminal dealer will not likely come with warning labels, non-lethal dosages, or antidotes in case of overdose.

The drugs will tend to be more expensive than if they were legal since supply is artificially cut short compared to demand, and dealers will charge a premium given the higher risks they are taking with their illegal business. Illegal drugs are also more likely to be super-potent because the dealer has to transport a lot of contraband and needs it to be strong so he can fit it all in his vehicle. If you could get paid to smuggle a bunch of contraband across the border, would you smuggle bulky cases of light beer in a bunch of trucks, or would you try to concentrate your stash in smaller, more potent, packages and fewer trucks so you had more to sell and less chance of being noticed or caught?

Black markets make it harder for people to use drugs in *any* rational sense. People can use drugs *rationally*? Sure, provided people are not putting themselves at severe health risks and are able to function at doing the rest of what matters to them, which arguably describes most users. Many if not most drug consumers are medical or recreational users – most users are not addicts. When the War on Drugs began around 100 years ago, a dominant theory was that the chemicals in drugs caused people to become addicted. If you puffed one joint, or used opium even once, you were at grave risk of becoming a violent drug-controlled zombie. (I suggest hosting a movie night featuring the 1936 anti-marijuana propaganda film *Reefer Madness*. There will be laughs aplenty.) That was the belief, and some people still believe this, but the evidence does not support it. How so? When grandma gets hip replacement surgery, she is usually given diamorphine, aka *heroin*, as a painkiller. Yet we don't witness a torrent of sweet elderly ladies becoming post-surgical junkies. It is estimated that 20% of U.S. troops used heroin regularly during the Vietnam War, but 95% of those users quit within a year after coming home.[1]

A non-addicted user who knows how to dose drugs may still be acting unsafely to some degree, but at least he can avoid lethality if he knows the strength of what he is using. However, your friendly neighborhood illegal drug pusher likely doesn't provide accurate labels or any reliable guarantees that what he's selling is actually what it is. After all, there is no legal recourse if things go very wrong, and Mr. Pusher knows this. You can't sue him for giving you tainted drugs that make you sick. You could demand a refund, I suppose, though such attempts likely escalate the chance of your blood being shed. Making drugs illegal tends to select for the hardest core of dishonest and violent suppliers of those items, since those are the type of people willing to work outside the law.[2]

What's more, black markets make it harder for *irrational* users, such as many addicts, to know the dangers of what they are using. Addicts tend to consume larger amounts and are much more likely to overdose without the proper knowledge of what they are consuming. People who overdose may not go to the hospital for fear of shame or criminal prosecution, so they end up dying alone in often most unpleasant ways such as choking on their own vomit. When unhealthy behavior is illegal, it is more likely to be driven underground not just for fear of legal sanctions but also moral sanctions like shame. People are ostracized as criminals and hopeless losers rather than being seen with compassion and care. They end up flocking to their own, squatting in crack houses, sharing needles, selling their bodies, and not associating with the outside world of more "functional" people. This is not to say that many addicts are not at least partly to blame for the pain they cause others. However, many of these addicts are deprived of adequate opportunities, such as rehabilitation, and so they go with all they see life has left to offer. Their bad choices are rendered even worse than in a world of legal drugs.

Criminalization of drugs has also led to civil rights violations associated with enforcement of drug laws. They have to be enforced or else they are just pointless ink taking up space in law books, and clearly people aren't always going to obey laws they consider inconvenient or even unjustified.

People and pets have been shot and killed by police teams conducting no-knock raids, sometimes with scanty evidence of illegality, sometimes even on the wrong house.[3] Victims of such raids, who often live in high-crime neighborhoods, have thought they are being robbed, so they defend themselves and end up being shot. The War on Drugs has led to militarization of police in many vicinities. Police forces meant to protect peaceful citizens from aggression often become the aggressors themselves.[4] Why does the local police force need military-grade equipment such as tanks?

People arrested for drug-related offenses are often detained for long periods of time without an attorney. They often cannot afford an attorney to represent them, so they have to rely on overworked public defenders who often just settle on plea bargains because of overloaded dockets.[5] Some states have mandatory minimum sentencing laws, forcing judges to hand out multi-year prison sentences to people who were just trying to sell or purchase marijuana.[6]

The author has been pulled over several times with an out-of-state license plate, so that an officer could see whether he was transporting anything illegal. This is annoying, to say the least, but I am privileged in this respect not to be a racial minority in the United States, whereas profiling of African-Americans and Hispanics, and instances of excessive force, is a known phenomenon.[7]

Mass incarceration is not only because of drug arrests, but a significant number of inmates are imprisoned for possession or sale. Nonviolent offenders are then subject to the known poor conditions of many jails and prisons. Their lives are often ruined after release from prison, as they are saddled with a criminal record that stigmatizes them in the eyes of many potential employers. Unable to find meaningful work, many of them return to their drug abuse. The inflated expense and underground economy of illegal drugs turns some addicts into genuine criminals. It often leads them to engage in real criminal activity that they wouldn't otherwise do (stealing, selling child pornography, etc.).

And then there is civil asset forfeiture – if (say) a driver is found with a bunch of cash, sometimes the assumption of law enforcement is that the cash is for some kind of illegal transaction. People have had their money, cars, and other assets seized without any evidence of wrongdoing.[8] The process for reclaiming their property – if they even can – is often difficult and time-consuming. The cynical view is that drug laws are often a smokescreen for revenue extraction by government officials who don't actually care about eliminating drug activity.

Now perhaps all these bad things are lamentable consequences of drug laws, but are they the price we have to pay to keep people from harming themselves? What would be so great about drug legalization if the risk we run is much greater access to drugs? For starters, legalization allows greater access to withdrawal services for addicts who want to quit. When addicts don't have to drive their behavior underground, more people will know that these so-called "junkies" are among their own friends and family. Once people are less afraid or ashamed to admit their addictions, more help can reach more people. Knowing one's friends or family members are struggling with addiction can reduce hysteria and moral panics about some mysterious Other, some fictional evil and dangerous squadron of violent junkies. We saw the same with the recently growing cultural acceptance of homosexuality. With drug addiction, behavior not driven underground is behavior better tracked so that those most in need have more chances to connect with other human beings, to seek and get the appropriate help through interventions, therapy, and so forth.

Legalization may also *reduce* deaths. After all, most people don't intend to kill themselves by using opioids. On the other hand, we have seen increased levels of suicide by people whose doctors cut them off from prescription opioids. Don't prescriptions and the Food and Drug Administration (FDA) save lives? Sure, but perhaps not on balance. What is *not* seen are the people who die or suffer harm when they are not allowed to take certain prescription or experimental drugs. Either way, prescriptions aren't automatic safeguards. Xanax is approved by the FDA but hundreds of people die each year taking it. Perhaps prescriptions raise a false sense of security? "Oh, my doctor prescribed this, so it must be safe." Not necessarily. Opioids may have a genuine place in reducing post-surgical pain, or treating certain mental health disorders, but there is a growing consensus that doctors often overprescribe them, giving patients a few weeks' worth of painkillers when a few days' worth makes more sense. So the false sense of security prescriptions convey may actually lead to *more* danger, as those more prone to addiction end up actually becoming addicted to opioids.

Wild idea: what if drugs like Xanax were over-the-counter instead? The obvious worry is we would then see thousands more people dying since they can just go to CVS and get opioids about as easily as buying aspirin. Not necessarily. The makers of the drug might take many more pains to dose it properly for fear of being sued under tort law, or having a reputation as killers of those making bad choices. Irresponsible physicians are not quite getting the scrutiny or criticism that drug manufacturers deservedly get for their irresponsible business practices. Allowing prescription drugs to be sold over-the-counter may actually force drug companies to become more accountable since they can no longer blame physicians for reckless prescriptions.[9]

There is also a phenomenon known as "Baptists and Bootleggers".[10] This was seen during the U.S.'s alcohol prohibition in the 1920s. The "Baptists" were those who made a moral case for banning the sale of alcohol because they believed there was an epidemic of alcohol dependence, especially among working-class people. The claim was that there were too many bars, people were getting drunk to the detriment of their health and moral character, and they were spending too much money on booze. They say politics can make for odd bedfellows, so who do you think joined the Baptists in the call for alcohol prohibition? Yes, Bootleggers! Thuggish gangsters like the notorious Al Capone.

And why would gangsters have supported laws prohibiting alcohol? Clearly it's because they cared about our safety, right? Nah. It was so *they* would be the only ones running the booze racket. Without legal competitors, the gangsters basically had a monopoly on the (illegal) sale of alcohol, and they could mark up prices so that they made a much higher profit than if they had to legally sell it. But why did they do something they knew to be against the law? Because they're *gangsters*! By definition, outlaws work outside the law. Prohibition didn't make demand for alcohol go away, but it did make law-abiding suppliers go away. Basic economics: if demand still outpaces the smaller number of new (illegal) suppliers, what happens to the price of alcohol? What happens to the quality of the alcoholic beverages? The people whom Prohibition was most intended to help now were spending more money on sometimes literal poison.

This is just one example of how both moral and self-serving rationales can join forces to support prohibition for quite different reasons. Debatably, we can see this phenomenon in other areas. Many in the cosmetology industry lobby for extensive licensing requirements for things like hair-braiding. They claim to be doing so out of safety concerns for clients. The effect is to also price out poorer people who cannot afford to go through all the training for a license, which keeps out competition. Large banks often lobby for extensive financial regulations in the name of concern for protecting investors and depositors. Maybe their executives are genuinely concerned with protecting people, but the effect is also to keep out competition from smaller financial companies and banks who can't afford to comply with all the regulations. Taxi companies often lobby against ride-sharing apps like Lyft and Uber. The hotel industry lobbies against Airbnb. Many sit-down restaurants lobby against food trucks. Weight loss companies lobby to define obesity downward.

Some might say: "We just need to get the right people in charge, and then these problems will go away." That's a fine response, but the million-dollar question is how we can get those right people in charge when the incentives often select for people without clean motives. And even if we can find the right people, are the incentives in place for them to achieve the intended outcomes of a prohibition? Either way, why can't opponents of paternalism just as easily say: "People just need to make better choices, and then the problems of prohibition will go away because then we wouldn't need paternalistic laws in the first place"? If that's too easy a response, why isn't "we just need to find the right people" also too easy a response? Either way, bad choices are used as whipping boys to call for interventions that might make matters even worse than if people were left free to make bad choices.

To be fair, most contemporary defenders of paternalism are skeptical of alcohol and drug prohibition. Some support drug decriminalization if not outright legalization. Their focus is more on taxing or prohibiting items like cigarettes and trans fats (I'll discuss trans fats in the next section). So what about prohibiting cigarettes? Would we see anything comparable to the problems attending prohibition of alcohol and other drugs?

My hypothesis is that we would see similar sorts of problems. Many smokers have strong first-order preferences to continue smoking – even many who might wish to quit. These strong preferences lead to fairly widespread demand for nicotine. In the absence of a viable substitute, black markets should emerge to help meet this demand. They may not be as widespread as black markets in alcohol or cocaine, but it's an open question. When enough people want something badly enough, laws won't keep many people from trying to get it. In light of these concerns, perhaps paternalists would advocate heavily taxing cigarettes rather than outright prohibiting them. Taxes or price floors may be better than banning cigarettes, but to be effective the taxes or prices would need to be rather steep. The hope might then be that more and more people would be dissuaded from buying something so expensive, and we would see a gradual decline in the appeal of smoking until we reach a point where it is very marginal in the culture. Maybe then bans would be effective and avoid the negative effects of prohibition.

No doubt, tobacco cigarettes are perhaps the most dangerous mechanisms for nicotine delivery humans could have invented. Paternalists who insist they should be banned might consider new or continued legalization of less unsafe devices (e.g., Snus, patches, vapes) that may be comparably effective in providing their users the pleasures they get from nicotine. Legal access to less dangerous devices would not end the problems associated with smoking – as of this writing, for instance, we have seen several thousand illnesses and several dozen deaths associated with vaping.[11] However, these numbers are still dwarfed by the number of illnesses and deaths caused by cigarettes. The question should then be how we can reduce harm since we'll never eliminate it altogether. Allowing less dangerous devices – and allowing entrepreneurs to discover possibly even less dangerous ones over time – may lead the tobacco cigarette to a natural extinction without prohibiting it at all. Just a thought.

UNINTENDED CONSEQUENCES OF REGULATIONS

Incentives matter, and a second reason for concern about how laws or regulations actually work, despite good intentions, has to do with unintended consequences. I'll give a few examples, but you should write a paper on other things you might think of! Consider safety requirements for new ladders. Can you imagine how these requirements might make people less safe? How is that possible? Typically regulations make things cost more. A nice shiny ladder that is required to be as safe as possible will probably be more expensive than a disallowed run-of-the-mill ladder that isn't dangerous but is less safe (and less expensive). Maybe the safest ladder has stronger metal alloys or thicker bolts, which drives up its price and makes fewer people willing to pay for it than if it was just a new basic ladder. So what might these people do? Instead of buying a new and more expensive ladder, they use the rotting old piece of crap that has been in their sheds for years. They end up having more accidents as a result. Maybe this is just an odd fact about ladders but doesn't apply to other things. I'd be surprised if that were true, however. Why wouldn't the same principle hold for cars, toasters, blenders, lawn mowers, airplanes, etc.?

Another example of unintended consequences involves "sin" taxes on cigarettes, as was mentioned previously. The thought is that if we tax or raise the price of cigarettes, smokers will buy fewer of them. (I wonder if Badly-off Bob appreciates this when he is priced out of the market and can no longer afford a daily pack of cigarettes.) Anyway, some people may just pay more for the same amount of harm, so they are harmed more overall with the taxes in place.

Defenders of the tax assume people respond to incentives, but if so, then they're not the out-of-control addicts that some of those same defenders allege them to be. On the other hand, if they are unable to respond to incentives because their addiction runs so deep, why think the tax would have a positive effect on their behavior? And a steep nicotine tax might in fact have harmful effects on some of the worst off, such as recovering narcotic addicts and alcoholics. Rehab clinics often recommend tobacco smoking to reduce addicts' cravings for more dangerous substances. But making certain substances prohibitively expensive may encourage people to substitute worse things, or make people more liable to abuse other things. A frustrated smoker not allowed cigarettes may take up heavy drinking or narcotics. A tax (or a ban) doesn't just magically extinguish cravings or efforts to satisfy those cravings.

A third example involves the possible unintended consequences of requiring food providers to post calorie counts. Recall the licensing effect discussed in Chapter 5. A person at lunch notices that a salad is only 300 calories. They order the salad instead of getting the 500-calorie sandwich they usually get. Still hungry later that day, they mindlessly snack on 300 calories of chips when the sandwich would have left them satisfied until dinner. All the person really thinks about is how their lunch was so much healthier, so they don't think about how the chips could have done more damage. But they end up ingesting 100 extra calories than usual because salad is all that's at the front of their mind.

This is not to say that all regulations – including paternalistic ones – backfire. Far from it. We need regulations sometimes so that we can make informed choices, so that we can be confident the bridge below us won't collapse, and so forth. But not all regulations serve their intended purpose. Even if you think "There oughta be a law!" it doesn't follow that the law will work in the way you expect. People respond to incentives, whether consciously or unconsciously. They are not chess pieces that can be manipulated by the best-laid plans of lawmakers. The lesson to draw from these examples is that we shouldn't judge a law or policy by its intentions but rather by its outcomes. Does it work to achieve whatever well-intentioned goal it was set out to achieve? If not, it may be worse than no law or policy at all on the matter. The best kinds of regulations are ones that are sensitive to how people respond to the incentives those regulations put into place. Ones that don't track incentives well can do more harm than if people were left free to make bad choices.

Defenders of paternalism can agree with all of this, to be sure. In addition, they might argue that regulating or prohibiting things that lots of people strongly prefer may not be priorities. Instead, they might focus on harmful things that people won't really miss if they're banned. There aren't black markets in asbestos or red dye #2, after all.[12] A contemporary example is artificial trans fats once found in many processed foods, which are known to be quite harmful if ingested in enough quantities over time. The nice thing is that foods made with healthier substitutes, such as coconut oil, taste nearly indistinguishable from foods made with trans fats. So if hardly anyone would miss trans fats, what's the problem? Gangbangers won't be patrolling the streets of Los Angeles with illicit cans of Crisco. And in fact, many food industries had already begun reducing or eliminating trans fats voluntarily, perhaps in response to consumer demand and negative press. The trade-off has been a slight rise in price due to the shifts, but since overall food prices continue to decline, this blip should hardly be noticed. And people will be eating healthier (or less unhealthy) food.

I'd like to pause briefly to consider whether I've now capitulated to paternalists, at least a bit. The focus of this book has mainly been on micro-level interactions – interactions between individuals or small groups. I haven't focused much on policies that affect millions on a large scale. The situation could be different on this larger scale, where most people aren't even aware of trans fats and their health risks. So here a ban may be the most effective approach if we're facing widespread ignorance – perhaps it could be justified on soft paternalistic grounds given that very ignorance. But imagine some consumers who for some odd reason really prefer the taste of trans-fatty foods. Maybe it's all in their heads, but they swear that such foods just taste better, seem to keep longer, and so forth. Even if trans fats are generally banned, could there be exceptions for those who in fact want to consume them despite the known risks?

Perhaps not. For a prohibition to have teeth, it may be the case that exemptions must be rare or not at all. That being said, perhaps such prohibitions can be justified even to our trans-fat fans. How? Perhaps policymakers' rationale can be summarized as follows: "We're not banning trans fats for your sake.

Rather, we're trying to protect other people from unwittingly doing dangerous things. Unfortunately, this requires a general ban that includes you because there is no feasible freedom-respecting alternative that can effectively warn people on such a massive scale." This rationale may pass an Acceptability standard if, say, everyone is committed to accepting the principle that one function of laws and policies is to protect people from unwitting harms. Whatever the case, the rationale for banning trans fats need not be a *hard paternalistic* one.[13]

SO WHAT?

Paternalists might respond "Look, if the consequences of some paternalistic laws and policies are bad enough, this just means these laws and policies aren't feasible, not that they are wrong in principle. But the fact of possible misapplication or abuse is a feature of *all laws*, not just paternalistic ones." Sound familiar? We covered this issue briefly in Chapter 1, where Jason Hanna argues that although we should be alert to potential misapplication or abuse of paternalist laws, there's nothing distinctively problematic about them in this regard.

All laws are potentially subject to capture, so indeed all of these concerns might be relevant, but there are also concerns about all the non-paternalistic laws that we don't tend to question. Traffic laws might encourage officers to "police for profit" by pulling over somebody on a technicality (going one mile per hour over the speed limit, or parking four inches too close to an intersection). Property laws might sometimes benefit the stronger by allowing the wealthiest to find tax loopholes. And so forth. But we typically think it would be bad to do away with these laws altogether *merely* because they might be abused. Why not think the same way about paternalistic laws?

I think I have a response to this argument. Traffic, property, and contract laws are typically things almost all of us *need* to coordinate our expectations and resolve disputes. Universal education and a social safety net are also needed to provide resources to free and equal persons who otherwise cannot easily afford them. We need coordination and dispute resolution whatever our goals and values. Traffic lights and road rules make clear who has the right of way so we don't all cluster in an endless traffic jam. Note that we usually obey traffic laws even when we could have broken them without punishment. We have internalized these norms because we see them as needed and see that others typically obey them – and expect us to obey them as well. Property rules let neighbors know what belongs to whom, and what happens when (say) a tree falls across their shared fence. Contract laws determine what promises are enforceable between the parties to the contract, and what is to happen if one party breaches the agreement. Contracts allow us to have things in writing so that, if a dispute arises, a weaker party can offer evidence to an impartial judge that wins him the case. All these rules and laws allow us to form expectations and plan ahead for the long term.

Without such laws and policies, many people would not know how to proceed in many cases, and disputes could boil over into deep resentment if not violence. The absence of such laws and policies would also make it much less likely for people to coordinate on complex and long-term projects, especially if they lacked a way of knowing that others would credibly act in trustworthy ways. Absence of such laws also hinders economic growth that can benefit everyone. In addition, redistributive policies can allow the worse off to have enough resources to pursue a decent life and not be disproportionately burdened by the obligations of living in society. Education policies may be needed to allow people the skills to be civil and productive members of the community.

However, it is far from clear that we need state-enforced *paternalistic* laws or policies in any similar way. Sure, some would *prefer to* have such laws, but an absence of such laws does not suggest the potential chaos that an absence of traffic, property, and contract laws might suggest. For some people – CADets and perhaps some Middle People – *no* hard paternalistic law at all is preferable to any hard paternalistic law. For almost all people some property law – even a law they're not crazy about but which does good enough for them – is preferable to no property law at all. I might have an odd preference to drive on the left side of the road, but I'm fine with driving on the right side of the road if that's what everyone else is doing. I might prefer property laws that don't allow for noise permits, but I'm willing to accept laws that allow such permits if I see them as proceeding from legitimate institutions needed to solve our disputes.

Again, there may be lots of space to make bad choices if trying to stop them brings more pain than it's worth.

Eight

I have tried to make a strong case against hard paternalistic laws and policies, but I hope to reiterate that not all hard paternalism is wrong, just that we have to be careful. Laws are blunt tools, whereas our private interactions often provide context, flexibility, and local knowledge. As a stranger, I can temporarily restrain Reckless Hiker from crossing a bridge he knows might be dangerous. As a friend, I can temporarily hide the bottle of whiskey from Drunk Buddy, perhaps even when I'm at his house. If, however, he gets mad at me when sober and tells me never to hide his booze again, I should respect his wishes. As a partner, I can hide the cookies from Mindlessly Snacking Husband and perhaps continue hiding them *even* if he finds it annoying. That depends on how we've defined the boundaries of our marriage. The particular details of our situations and relationships – details that might make paternalism seem more palatable – are usually too fine-grained and complex for general laws to handle. As a summary:

I argued in Chapter 1 that it's OK to make bad choices if they aren't sufficiently harmful, and that even defenders of paternalism can agree about this. We should have ample space to experiment and learn from our mistakes when not too much is at stake. Harms may be severe, or immediate, or irreversible – or some combination – but I argued that harms which have only one of these features should not typically be subject to hard paternalism, and paternalists typically agree with this. I then surveyed some of the most powerful arguments in favor of paternalism by showing that many standard objections to them aren't convincing. My hope is that the arguments I laid out in this book can make up for the deficiencies in these standard objections.

I argued in Chapter 2 that many "bad" choices aren't actually bad, and so they are OK too. Again, defenders of paternalism may agree with this assessment since they accept that welfare should be understood subjectively, mostly as a matter of what best satisfies our preferences and goals. That being said, since outside observers lack reliable access to what goes on in people's minds, they are often ill-prepared to make confident judgments about whether people's choices truly reflect their preferences. In such cases, perhaps we should take people's actions as most reflective of what they want, regardless of what they might say or even pay. *It's OK to make "bad" choices that aren't actually or clearly bad.*

I argued in Chapter 3 that people may sometimes make bad free choices that don't truly reflect their own preferences, beliefs, and values. Here is where I now part ways with most paternalists, who defend the view that it may then be OK to interfere with such people. By contrast, I argue that some people may still want the freedom to make bad choices even if those choices don't align with those people's preferences, beliefs, and values. I discussed CADets at some length to drive home the point that some people may want freedom from paternalism *even though* coercion may promote or protect their other interests. *It's legally OK to make bad choices when you believe that having the freedom to make bad choices adds value to your freely making good choices.*

Why It's OK to Make Bad Choices

In Chapter 4, I argued that defenders of paternalism should not assume pro-paternalism is the default view in the absence of a prior commitment to CAD. As with any view, people should have decisive reason to accept the rationale for coercion (paternalist or otherwise) – merely lacking decisive reason to reject the rationale isn't enough to avoid the coercer substituting her judgment for that of the equal person she coerces. It's legally OK to make bad choices when it's not OK for another to force her pro-paternalist judgment on you.

In Chapter 5, I argued that some bad choices may not be OK if they're not sufficiently free or if we lack sufficient evidence that they are free. In those cases, soft paternalism may be in order since almost everyone presumably doesn't want to make bad decisions over which they might not even know they lack control. I also discussed how in some cases, rather than relying on ourselves entirely to deal with cognitive or motivational biases, we can make better choices through exposure to choice-preserving nudges.

I argued in Chapter 6 that it may be legally OK to make bad choices provided they don't place undue costs on others. Since we in a liberal democracy don't want to arbitrarily select certain valued freedoms over others, perhaps the best approach is to absorb any social costs through a mandatory social insurance scheme where people pay on a sliding scale.

Finally, in Chapter 7 I argued that it's legally OK to make bad choices if efforts to prohibit them would likely raise more costs than the efforts are worth. But have I at any point argued that it's any more than legally OK to make actually bad choices? I should close with some thoughts on that. I've hinted at it throughout the book but didn't go into much more detail because my sense is that we all understand why it's important to have lots of chances to learn from our mistakes.

Sometimes we don't know a choice is bad until after we've made it. We live under risk and uncertainty. We are inherently subject to luck, good and bad. We are human. If a person doesn't know when many of his choices will end up being good or bad, how can we know? How can laws know? Maybe Well-off Wynn meets a fellow smoker and falls in love, and both of them quit within a few years. Maybe she never falls in love and gets cancer in her 40s even without the genetic predisposition for it. Maybe Physicist Phil would have met the love of his life . . . had he chosen to stay alive. We'll never know for sure.

We can learn from mistakes, our own or others. It may be bad for me to make certain choices, but others can learn from my tribulations. I might see another person's bad choices – his drug habit or the poor way he treats other people – and tell myself that I'm never going to act the way he acts, that I'm not That Guy. Wisdom often results from screwing up. Wisdom is also about learning from bad choices, not making the same bad ones over and over. Of course, it's not *always* OK to make bad choices – that wasn't the title of this book!

However, we should be careful about being too careful. At least, we should be careful about making others be more careful than *they* might want to be. Not everyone prefers the same level of safety, so we shouldn't impose our preferred level on them without very good reason that they would see as justified. For the reasons I have explored in this book, their lives are not ours to decide. Alas, if there are to be hard paternalistic laws, will they be pretty rare or will they be abundant? If rare, it might make the case harder for why we need *any* if the arguments here are plausible. If abundant, then we run the risk of imposing a much more oppressive system on ourselves, and concerns about the "Nanny State" ring truer.

Our imperfection is part of what makes this journey at times touching, at times comedic, at times tragic, at times inspiring. One need not be religious to think that redemption can play a key role in the narrative of a life. Learning from bad choices, but either way having the freedom to make them, is part of being human and being able to lead a life of one's own. I've made numerous mistakes over the course of thinking about these matters. I feel confident that I've made a strong case against paternalism, but I could still be wrong. That's for you to judge. I hope my experience has given you some ideas to consider in your own lives. Godspeed.

Notes

WHAT THE *BLEEP* DO WE KNOW?

1 Richard Thaler and Cass Sunstein, *Nudge: Improving Decisions About Health, Wealth, and Happiness* (New York: Penguin, 2009).

2 By "lovely" Smith didn't exactly mean being endearing or physically pretty, though those elements might be involved. Rather, he meant having a character worthy of admiration and love. Obviously, not everyone will agree that this is a desire most people have. What do you think?

3 Jason Hanna, *In Our Best Interest* (Oxford: Oxford University Press, 2018), p. 4.

4 Ibid.

5 Ibid., p. 44.

6 "[E]ven if individuality is an element of well-being, it is surely not the only element of well-being, and it may be worth sacrificing some individuality for the sake of other goods. Such tradeoffs would be ruled out only if one were to assign a very strong form of priority to individuality." Hanna, *In Our Best Interest*, p. 48.

7 Ibid., p. 51.

8 Ibid., pp. 52–53.

9 "Pro-paternalism . . . does not presuppose any particular theory of well-being. It can thus accommodate the claim that individuality is a component of well-being. Suppose it is. Suppose further that intervention in the self-regarding sphere would virtually always inhibit individuality without advance other, more important interests. The conclusion we should then draw is that liberty-limiting intervention in a person's self-regarding choices can only rarely be justified. The claim that the pro-paternalist view would only rarely justify intervention, however, does not show that it is false." Hanna, *In Our Best Interest*, p. 48.

10 For a thorough discussion of slippery slope concerns in policymaking, see Mario Rizzo and Douglas Glen Whitman, "Little Brother Is Watching You: New Paternalism on the Slopes," *Arizona Law Review* 51 (2009): 685.

11 Sarah Conly, *Against Autonomy: Justifying Coercive Paternalism* (Cambridge: Cambridge University Press, 2012), p. 33.

12 Ibid., p. 88.

13 "Most of us accept [mandatory safety equipment] because we believe that this increase in safety outweighs any associated costs. According to the view I defend, things are no different in those contexts more commonly thought to raise concerns about paternalism." Hanna, *In Our Best Interest*, p. 5.

14 Conly, *Against Autonomy*, p. 2.

15 Sarah Conly, "Three Cheers for the Nanny State," www.nytimes.com/2013/03/25/opinion/three-cheers-for-the-nanny-state.html

16 Conly, *Against Autonomy*, p. 3. Emphasis added.

17 Ibid.

18 Ibid., p. 72.

19 Ibid., p. 90.

20 Ibid., p. 93.

21 Ibid., p. 95.

22 Ibid., p. 91.

23 Ibid., p. 184.

24 Ibid.

25 Note that Hanna has similar reservations about paternalism through legal coercion. He doesn't oppose it in principle, but he writes "[A]lthough the fact that some policy would deter imprudent behavior is always a valid reason in favor of intervention, it is not always a decisive reason." Hanna, *In Our Best Interest*, p. 6.

HOW DO WE KNOW WHAT OTHER PEOPLE ARE UP TO?

1 Mark D. White, *The Manipulation of Choice* (New York: Palgrave Macmillan, 2013), pp. ix, xiv.

2 Rizzo and Whitman, "Little Brother Is Watching You," p. 423.

3 Thaler and Sunstein, *Nudge*, p. 5.

4 See Douglas Glen Whitman and Mario J. Rizzo, "The Problematic Welfare Standards of Behavioral Paternalism," *Review of Philosophy and Psychology* 6(3) (2015): 409–425.

5 Christopher Cherniak, *Minimal Rationality* (Cambridge: MIT Press, 1986). In contrast with this idealizing stance, Cherniak finds evidence of optimal wiring in the mammalian cerebral cortex – shortcuts and energy-savers in processing information that is "good enough" even if it departs from the "ideally rational" assuming no such processing costs.

6 Robert Sugden, "Why Incoherent Preferences Do Not Justify Paternalism," *Constitutional Political Economy* 19(3) (2008): 226–248, 232.

7 Thaler and Sunstein, *Nudge*, p. 243.

8 Oren Bar-Gill and Elizabeth Warren, "Making Credit Safer," *University of Pennsylvania Law Review* 157(1) (2008): 1–101 at pp. 33–43. On transaction costs, see Joshua D. Wright and Douglas H. Ginsburg, "Behavioral Law and Economics: Its Origins, Fatal Flaws, and Implications for Liberty," *Northwestern University Law Review* 106 (2015): 62–67.

9 Whitman and Rizzo, "The Problematic Welfare Standards of Behavioral Paternalism," 409–425.

10 Some people even have dispositions to be impulsive and engage in risky behavior. These people who abide by the credo "live fast and die young" don't will themselves harm, of course, but the kinds of excitement they indulge in bring attendant chances of an early death. Does this make their risk preferences or relatively high time discount rates "incorrect"? Limiting cases can certainly obtain: given any reasonable evaluative standards, it's probably irrational to prefer 1 hour of life at 50.1 average utiles over a lifetime at 50 average utiles. But what about 40 years of life at 60 average utiles over 80 years of life at 50 average utiles? There's an old quip: "Nobody on their deathbed says they wish they had spent more time at the office."

11 Robert Nozick, *The Nature of Rationality* (Princeton, NJ: Princeton University Press, 1993), p. 16.

12 "Across a certain domain of possibilities, consumers will often lack well-formed preferences, in the sense of preferences that are firmly held. . . . If the arrangement of the alternatives has a significant effect on the selections the customers make, then their true 'preferences' do not formally exist" (Cass Sunstein and Thaler Richard, "Libertarian Paternalism Is Not an Oxymoron," *University of Chicago Law Review* 70 (2001): 1159–1202 at p. 1164).

13 Ibid., p. 1161.

14 White, *The Manipulation of Choice*, pp. 64–80.

15 Hanna, *In Our Best Interest*, p. 30.

WHAT IF I REALLY AM MAKING BAD CHOICES?

1 Harry Frankfurt, "Freedom of the Will and the Concept of a Person," *The Journal of Philosophy* 68(1) (1971): 5–20.

2 This is not to say that a novelist who accepted the uninvited alterations would necessarily be irrational. Perhaps he accepts the novel's success, whatever his own input, as a springboard to greater things.

3 See Stanley Benn, *A Theory of Freedom* (Cambridge: Cambridge University Press, 1988), pp. 11–15.

4 The author's record is 19 in a row, which he still finds impressive, even though his friends don't seem to care.

5 Benn, *A Theory of Freedom*, p. 87.

YOU'RE NOT THE BOSS OF ME!

1 Charles Larmore, *The Morals of Modernity* (Cambridge: Cambridge University Press, 1993).
2 John Rawls, *Political Liberalism* (New York: Columbia University Press, 1993), pp. 54–58.
3 Gilbert Harman, *Reasoning, Meaning, and Mind* (Oxford: Oxford University Press, 1999), p. 23.
4 Roy F. Baumeister and John Tierney, *Willpower: Rediscovering the Greatest Human Strength* (New York: Penguin, 2011), pp. 43–60.
5 Ibid., pp. 88–107.
6 I say "sufficiently informed" because "completely informed" is impossible and perhaps *undesirable*. In our world of scarce resources, there are opportunity costs in gathering each additional increment of information under uncertainty of its merits, not to mention the cognitive energy expended in such a search. Exhaustion could set in – imagine the thinking equivalent of hitting the gym right after running a marathon. So we can't assume the *cost* of obtaining each additional increment of information is less than the uncertain *benefits* of having each additional increment. At some point the additional costs outweigh the additional benefits, and often we even lack information about the point at which those net costs begin. Reasoning is possibly a never-ending process in which our state of limited cognitive ability *emphasizes* the relevance of an Acceptability standard.

BIASES AND SOFT PATERNALISM

1 Art Markman, "Your Future Happiness Depends Less on the Present Than You Might Think," www.psychologytoday.com/us/blog/ulterior-motives/201011/your-future-happiness-depends-less-the-present-you-might-think?collection=80437
2 See Kalle Grill, "Respect for What? Choices, Actual Preferences, and True Preferences," *Social Theory and Practice* 41(4) (October 2015): 692–715.
3 Kathleen D. Vohs, et al., "Making Choices Impairs Subsequent Self-Control: A Limited Resource Account of Decision Making, Self-Regulation, and Active Initiative," *Journal of Personality and Social Psychology* 94 (2008): 883–898.
4 For a popular treatment of this topic, see Barry Schwartz, *The Paradox of Choice* (New York: Harper Perennial, 2004).
5 W.K. Bickel and M.W. Johnson, "Delay Discounting: A Fundamental Behavioral Process of Drug Dependence," in G. Loewenstein, D. Read and R. Baumeister, eds., *Time and Decision* (New York: Russell Sage, 2003), pp. 419–440.

6 Timothy A. Pychyl, "Procrastination: It's Not Me, It's the Situation!", www.psychologytoday.com/blog/dont-delay/200803/procrastination-its-not-me-its-the-situation

7 Timothy A. Pychyl, "I'll Just Check My Email, It Will Only Take a Minute," www.psychologytoday.com/blog/dont-delay/200803/ill-just-check-my-email-it-will-only-take-minute

8 Timothy A. Pychyl, "Evaluation Threat and Procrastination," www.psychologytoday.com/blog/dont-delay/200805/evaluation-threat-and-procrastination

9 I made a commitment to a friend that we wouldn't grab a beer until I turned in this manuscript. As of this writing, she has held me to it.

10 J. Kruger and D. Dunning, "Unskilled and Unaware of It: How Difficulties in Recognizing One's Own Incompetence Leads to Inflated Self-Assessments," *Journal of Personality and Social Psychology* 77 (1999): 1121–1134.

11 Psychology Research and Reference, "Belief Perseverance," https://psychology.iresearchnet.com/social-psychology/social-cognition/belief-perseverance/

12 Baumeister and Tierney, *Willpower*, p. 122.

13 Some states have "self-exclusion" programs for people who want to stop gambling. They can voluntarily put themselves on a publicly shared list where casinos are required not to allow them in or cash any winnings. For an example from Kansas, see: www.krgc.ks.gov/index.php/responsible-gambling/voluntary-exclusion-program

14 Ibid., p. 136.

15 Daniel A. Marano, "Nature's Bounty: License to Fill," www.psychologytoday.com/articles/200909/natures-bounty-license-fill

16 J.C. Witt Huberts, C. Evers and D.T.D. De Ridder, "License to Sin: Self-licensing as a Mechanism Underlying Hedonic Consumption," *European Journal of Social Psychology* 42 (2012): 490–496. doi: 10.1002/ejsp.861

KEEP YOUR BAD CHOICES OUT OF MY BANK ACCOUNT!

1 For an excellent defense of anti-perfectionist liberalism, see Jonathan Quong, *Liberalism Without Perfection* (Oxford: Oxford University Press, 2011).

2 See, for instance, Jan J. Barendregt, et al., "The Health Care Costs of Smoking," *New England Journal of Medicine* 337(15) (1997 October 9): 1052–1057.

3 But even then there may be cases where, say, eating chips does play a significant role in someone's life. Perhaps they are the most vivid way to remind one of a partner, now deceased, with whom one used to engage in the activity. A defender of the restrictive view could make a case for exempting people from restrictions in such cases, although

space considerations prevent me from exploring how those exemptions might work.

4 I am grateful to [omitted] for suggesting this.

5 I am grateful to [omitted] for suggesting this possibility.

6 An anonymous reviewer asks why it is unjust if poorer people can't afford mandatory "risky freedom insurance" for certain activities if, for instance, it's not unjust when poorer people can't afford expensive activities like skiing. Here is my attempt at a reply: with the latter, presumably no other person or group is responsible for my expensive taste and inability to pay. However, let's say I can afford skis but not mandatory insurance at its normal rate. I would be free to ski but for other people restricting me and imposing an obligation to buy insurance in order to ski. Because of this costly obligation demanded of me, perhaps they are in turn obligated to charge premiums on a sliding scale. What would otherwise be a bad choice (bad in the sense of placing undue costs on others) might become less bad or otherwise permissible because insurance would make it less costly to others through pooling risk.

7 Why not instead have sales or "sin" taxes on socially costly behaviors in addition to, or instead of, mandatory insurance? A major fairness concern is that such taxes would disproportionately burden the worst off since they are regressive – poorer people would pay a larger percentage of their wealth or income than would richer people. Do you agree or disagree that this would be unfair?

WHY WE SHOULD BE CAREFUL

1 Johann Hari, *Chasing the Scream* (New York: Bloomsbury, 2015), p. 173.

2 Jeffrey A. Miron, https://scholar.harvard.edu/files/miron/files/budget_2010_final_0.pdf

3 Bill Chappell, "Houston Police To Cease 'No-Knock' Warrants, Chief Announces After Deadly Raid," www.npr.org/2019/02/19/695926963/houston-police-to-cease-no-knock-warrants-chief-announces-after-deadly-raid

4 Radley Balko, *Rise of the Warrior Cop: The Militarization of America's Police Forces* (New York: PublicAffairs, 2013).

5 Emily Yoffe, "Innocence Is Irrelevant," www.theatlantic.com/magazine/archive/2017/09/innocence-is-irrelevant/534171/

6 Nancy Gertner and Chiraag Bains, "Mandatory Minimum Sentences Are Cruel and Ineffective: Sessions Wants Them Back," www.washingtonpost.com/posteverything/wp/2017/05/15/mandatory-minimum-sentences-are-cruel-and-ineffective-sessions-wants-them-back/

7 Ranjana Natarajan, "Racial Profiling Has Destroyed Public Trust In Police: Cops Are Exploiting Our Weak Laws Against It," www.washingtonpost.

com/posteverything/wp/2014/12/15/racial-profiling-has-de
stroyed-public-trust-in-police-cops-are-exploiting-our-weak-laws-
against-it/

8 https://ij.org/wp-content/uploads/2015/11/policing-for-profit-
2nd-edition.pdf

9 See Jessica Flanigan, *Pharmaceutical Freedom* (Oxford: Oxford University
Press, 2017).

10 Adam C. Smith and Bruce Yandle, *Bootleggers and Baptists: How Economic Forces
and Moral Persuasion Interact to Shape Regulatory Politics* (Washington, DC: Cato
Institute, 2014).

11 Centers for Disease Control and Prevention, "Outbreak of Lung Injury
Associated With the Use of Vaping, or E-Cigarette, Products," www.cdc.
gov/tobacco/basic_information/e-cigarettes/severe-lung-disease.html

12 I am grateful to an anonymous referee for pressing me to consider this
point.

13 The whole issue of bans may be made obsolete if the market accom-
modates consumer demand for comparably priced and quality non-
trans-fatty foods. Presumably, consumers don't want something that
has comparable benefits but higher costs than a competing food that is
much less unhealthy. Likewise, producers don't want to produce unsafe
foods (for fear of lawsuits or bad reputations) if less unsafe but otherwise comparable foods are available. This can explain why many food
producers voluntarily stopped using trans fats before any bans were
passed. This observation might be generalized to other sorts of unsafe
items (such as asbestos) that people don't miss given the availability of
safer substitutes.

References

Balko, Radley, *Rise of the Warrior Cop: The Militarization of America's Police Forces* (New York: PublicAffairs, 2013)

Barendregt, Jan J., et al., "The Health Care Costs of Smoking," *New England Journal of Medicine* 337(15) (1997 October 9): 1052–1057

Bar-Gill, Oren and Elizabeth Warren, "Making Credit Safer," *University of Pennsylvania Law Review* 157(1) (2008)

Baumeister, Roy F. and John Tierney, *Willpower: Rediscovering the Greatest Human Strength* (New York: Penguin, 2011)

Benn, Stanley, *A Theory of Freedom* (Cambridge: Cambridge University Press, 1988)

Bickel, W.K. and M.W. Johnson, "Delay Discounting: A Fundamental Behavioral Process of Drug Dependence," in G. Loewenstein, D. Read and R. Baumeister, eds., *Time and Decision* (New York: Russell Sage, 2003)

Carpenter, Dick M. II, et al., "Policing for Profit: The Abuse of Civil Asset Forfeiture," 2nd edition: https://ij.org/wp-content/uploads/2015/11/policing-for-profit-2nd-edition.pdf

Centers for Disease Control and Prevention, "Outbreak of Outbreak of Lung Injury Associated with the Use of E-Cigarette, or Vaping, Products": www.cdc.gov/tobacco/basic_information/e-cigarettes/severe-lung-disease.html

Chappell, Bill, "Houston Police to Cease 'No-Knock' Warrants, Chief Announces After Deadly Raid": www.npr.org/2019/02/19/695926963/houston-police-to-cease-no-knock-warrants-chief-announces-after-deadly-raid

Cherniak, Christopher, *Minimal Rationality* (Cambridge: MIT Press, 1986)

Conly, Sarah, *Against Autonomy: Justifying Coercive Paternalism* (Cambridge: Cambridge University Press, 2012)

Conly, Sarah, "Three Cheers for the Nanny State": www.nytimes.com/2013/03/25/opinion/three-cheers-for-the-nanny-state.html

Flanigan, Jessica, *Pharmaceutical Freedom* (Oxford: Oxford University Press, 2017)

Frankfurt, Harry, "Freedom of the Will and the Concept of a Person," *The Journal of Philosophy* 68(1) (1971)

Gertner, Nancy and Chiraag Bains, "Mandatory Minimum Sentences Are Cruel And Ineffective: Sessions Wants Them Back": www.washingtonpost.com/posteverything/wp/2017/05/15/mandatory-minimum-sentences-are-cruel-and-ineffective-sessions-wants-them-back/

Grill, Kalle, "Respect for What? Choices, Actual Preferences, and True Preferences," *Social Theory and Practice* 41(4) (October 2015)

Hanna, Jason, *In Our Best Interest* (Oxford: Oxford University Press, 2018)

Hari, Johann, *Chasing the Scream* (New York: Bloomsbury, 2015)

Harman, Gilbert, *Reasoning, Meaning, and Mind* (Oxford: Oxford University Press, 1999)

Kansas Racing and Gaming Commission, "Voluntary Exclusion": www.krgc.ks.gov/index.php/responsible-gambling/voluntary-exclusion-program

Kruger, J. and D. Dunning, "Unskilled and Unaware of It: How Difficulties in Recognizing One's Own Incompetence Leads to Inflated Self-Assessments," *Journal of Personality and Social Psychology* 77 (1999)

Larmore, Charles, *The Morals of Modernity* (Cambridge: Cambridge University Press, 1993)

Marano, Daniel A., "Nature's Bounty: License to Fill": www.psychologytoday.com/us/articles/200909/natures-bounty-license-fill

Markman, Art, "Your Future Happiness Depends Less on the Present Than You Might Think": www.psychologytoday.com/us/blog/ulterior-motives/201011/your-future-happiness-depends-less-the-present-you-might-think?collection=80437

Miron, Jeffrey A.: https://scholar.harvard.edu/files/miron/files/budget_2010_final_0.pdf

Natarajan, Ranjana, "Racial Profiling Has Destroyed Public Trust In Police: Cops Are Exploiting Our Weak Laws Against It": www.washingtonpost.com/posteverything/wp/2014/12/15/racial-profiling-has-destroyed-public-trust-in-police-cops-are-exploiting-our-weak-laws-against-it/

No author found, "Belief Perseverance": https://psychology.iresearchnet.com/social-psychology/social-cognition/belief-perseverance/

Nozick, Robert, *The Nature of Rationality* (Princeton, NJ: Princeton University Press, 1993)

Pychyl, Timothy A., "Evaluation Threat and Procrastination": www.psychologytoday.com/blog/dont-delay/200805/evaluation-threat-and-procrastination

Pychyl, Timothy A., "I'll Just Check My Email, It Will Only Take a Minute . . .": www.psychologytoday.com/blog/dont-delay/200803/ill-just-check-my-email-it-will-only-take-minute

Why It's OK to Make Bad Choices

Pychyl, Timothy A., "Procrastination: It's Not Me, It's the Situation!": www.psychologytoday.com/blog/dont-delay/200803/procrastination-its-not-me-its-the-situation

Quong, Jonathan, *Liberalism Without Perfection* (Oxford: Oxford University Press, 2011)

Rawls, John, *Political Liberalism* (New York: Columbia University Press, 1993)

Rizzo, Mario and Douglas Glen Whitman, "Little Brother Is Watching You: New Paternalism on the Slopes," *Arizona Law Review* 51 (2009): 685

Schwartz, Barry, *The Paradox of Choice* (New York: Harper Perennial, 2004)

Smith, Adam C. and Bruce Yandle, *Bootleggers and Baptists: How Economic Forces and Moral Persuasion Interact to Shape Regulatory Politics* (Washington, DC: Cato Institute, 2014)

Sugden, Robert, "Why Incoherent Preferences Do Not Justify Paternalism," *Constitutional Political Economy* 19(3) (2008): 226–248

Sunstein, Cass and Richard Thaler, "Libertarian Paternalism Is Not an Oxymoron," *University of Chicago Law Review* 70 (2001)

Thaler, Richard and Cass Sunstein, *Nudge: Improving Decisions About Health, Wealth, and Happiness* (New York: Penguin, 2009)

Vohs, Kathleen D., et al., "Making Choices Impairs Subsequent Self-Control: A Limited Resource Account of Decision Making, Self-Regulation, and Active Initiative," *Journal of Personality and Social Psychology* 94 (2008)

White, Mark D., *The Manipulation of Choice* (New York: Palgrave Macmillan, 2013)

Whitman, Douglas Glen and Mario J. Rizzo, "The Problematic Standards of Behavioral Paternalism," *Review of Philosophy and Psychology* 6(3) (2015): 409–425

Witt Huberts, J.C., C. Evers and D.T.D. De Ridder, "License to Sin: Self-licensing as a Mechanism Underlying Hedonic Consumption," *European Journal of Social Psychology* 42 (2012): 490–496. doi:10.1002/ejsp.861

Wright, Joshua D. and Douglas H. Ginsburg, "Behavioral Law and Economics: Its Origins, Fatal Flaws, and Implications for Liberty," *Northwestern University Law Review* 106 (2015): 1033

Yoffe, Emily, "Innocence Is Irrelevant": www.theatlantic.com/magazine/archive/2017/09/innocence-is-irrelevant/534171/

For Product Safety Concerns and Information please contact our EU
representative GPSR@taylorandfrancis.com
Taylor & Francis Verlag GmbH, Kaufingerstraße 24, 80331 München, Germany